Cynthia Owen grew up in [...] school, said her prayers and took her first communion with all the other girls in her class. But behind the façade of respectability lurked a hideous reality.

Cynthia was just eight years old when she was sexually abused by her father amongst others. Shortly before her eleventh birthday she was made pregnant and, minutes after giving birth to the baby, Cynthia watched in horror as her own mother murdered the tiny infant, named Noleen, by repeatedly stabbing her with a knitting needle. Cynthia's mother then wrapped the baby girl in a plastic bag, dumped her in an alleyway and made her daughter go back to school and pretend nothing had ever happened.

After enduring many more years of rape and violence, Cynthia came forward and reported her abuse and Noleen's death.

Finally, in 2007, after a fifteen-year legal fight to have her baby girl formally identified, the jury at the 'Dun Laoghaire Baby' inquest declared that the baby found dead in an alleyway thirty-four years previously was Noleen Murphy, the daughter of Cynthia Owen.

Cynthia's is a horrific story of brutality and loss, but ultimately, it is an account of love, immense bravery and her fight for justice in Noleen's name.

Cynthia Owen is happily married and lives in the UK.
Living With Evil is her first book.

Living With Evil

CYNTHIA OWEN

headline
review

First published in 2010
by HEADLINE REVIEW
An imprint of Headline Publishing Group

First published in paperback in 2010
by HEADLINE REVIEW

2

Cataloguing in Publication Data is available from the British Library

ISBN 978 0 7553 1905 3

Typeset in Monotype Dante by Ellipsis Books Limited, Glasgow

Printed and bound in Great Britain by
Clays Ltd, St Ives plc

Headline's policy is to use papers that are natural, renewable
and recyclable products and made from wood grown in sustainable forests.
The logging and manufacturing processes are expected to conform to
the environmental regulations of the country of origin.

HEADLINE PUBLISHING GROUP
An Hachette UK Company
338 Euston Road
London NW1 3BH

www.headline.co.uk
www.hachette.co.uk

This book is dedicated to my daughter, Noleen, to my sister Theresa and my brothers Martin and Michael, and for all victims of sexual abuse and violence. And to women who have become pregnant by their abusers. My wish for you is that this book brings you hope.

This is my story, told through my eyes. I am telling the story of what I saw, what happened to me and what my dead siblings, Theresa and Martin, told me happened to them too. I have not included other people's account of events. It is their right to tell their own stories, this is mine. Although this is a work of fact, some of the names of people and places have been changed, as well as some descriptions of people and places.

Prologue

'Have you reached a decision?'

The coroner's voice made my heart skip a beat, and silence fell as the foreman of the jury stood up.

'Twelve agree that it is Cynthia Owen's baby.'

I broke down completely. I felt eleven-years-old again. My baby had just died.

'Twelve agree that it was 4 April 1973.'

The words danced in my head. I had finally proved I wasn't mad, and I wasn't a liar.

I was forty-five-years old, and I had a daughter who would be almost thirty-four-years old, had she lived.

'Twelve agree the place of death was 4 White's Villas, Dalkey.

'Cause of death: haemorrhage due to stab wounds. Twelve agree. An open verdict.'

The room erupted. People started clapping and shouting, 'Yes!', at the top of their voices. I felt like a volt of electricity was coursing through my body.

I took the stand, barely able to support myself on my shaking legs, and the room fell silent again.

'Mrs Owen, I believe you have given your baby a first name, is that correct?'

'Yes,' I whispered.

'And what is that name?'

'Noleen.'

Her name hung in the thick silence for a moment, then I listened, awestruck, as the coroner said he was officially identifying the baby found in Lee's Lane on Wednesday 4 April 1973 as my daughter, Noleen Murphy, stabbed to death in my family home.

I looked at the jury and mouthed, 'Thank you,' then dropped into my husband Simon's lap and broke down into loud, unruly sobs.

When I finally staggered outside I looked up at the clear sky and smiled broadly. I had waited so long for this day to come, and I could scarcely believe it was real.

'Rest in peace, my darling Noleen,' I whispered up to heaven. 'Mummy loves you.'

I would like to be able to tell you that my battle to be formally identified as Noleen's mother and to have the details of her short life publicly recorded was the worst struggle I faced after the trauma of losing her, but sadly that is not the case.

I faced many more nightmares, each one testing me to the

limit and threatening to push me over the edge. If it hadn't been for my wonderful husband, Simon, I am certain I would not have survived.

Thanks to his unconditional love and support, I am alive and well, and able to tell the rest of my story.

Chapter 1

4 White's Villas

I'm eight-years-old and in bed waiting for Daddy to come in from the pub, and I'm trembling.

Mammy forced me upstairs to bed hours ago, but I can't sleep. I'm in my vest and knickers, huddled under dirty coats and smelly blankets, and I'm terrified about what will happen tonight.

Daddy always comes in when it's very dark, but that is the only thing I can be sure of. When I hear his leather shoes crunching up the short path to our council house, my heart starts to thump in my chest.

Sometimes I say a prayer, pressing my hands together tight like the nuns at school taught me: 'Please, God, please can it be a good night tonight? I've been a very good girl, so I have.'

Daddy usually goes straight to the pub after work and drinks and smokes all night with his friends. The pubs are near our house in Dalkey, and sometimes he can take in three or four in one evening, depending on his mood.

Mammy always stays in our house at 4 White's Villas. Every night she rocks in her chair by the coal fire, drinking glass after glass of sherry and lighting one cigarette from another.

When Daddy gets home, sometimes they shout and scream if they have both had lots to drink, but sometimes he doesn't even speak to her.

I'm listening hard, but I'm so nervous I start breathing really quickly, and I'm gasping noisily for breath. It feels like I'm being strangled, but it's just the fear choking me and making it hard for the air to fill my lungs.

It sounds quiet downstairs, and that is normally a good sign. Daddy is ignoring Mammy, and she's not speaking either. That's very good. I hate it when I hear their voices get louder, because then the fights and arguments start.

It scares me, because when Daddy is cross it usually means bad things for me. Despite the good signs, I still can't relax. I listen out for sounds that tell me he is on his way upstairs. I never know what he's going to do, and every time I hear the bedroom door open I start to shake.

Daddy's in the room now. I hear him use the toilet bucket at the end of the bed. The smell is terrible. It makes my eyes sting even when I'm hiding under the covers, and my stomach starts to churn so much it hurts.

There's no lid on the bucket, and we never have anything

to put in it to make it smell better. We don't even have toilet paper.

I've buried myself deep under my covers, but I can't escape the stench. It seems to follow me, clinging to my skin and sticking in my throat. I can't get away from it.

I can hear Daddy stripping off his trousers. He always sleeps in just a shirt, or sometimes nothing at all.

My throat goes very dry now, and I'm trying to pretend I'm fast asleep, even though I'm shaking so much the covers must be moving up and down, telling him I am wide awake.

Maybe Daddy will leave me alone tonight?

He wasn't staggering about like he does some nights, and he didn't shout at Mammy. Maybe he will fall into bed and start snoring loudly, giving me the sign that tonight I can go to sleep knowing he's too drunk to do those horrible things to me, that just for tonight, he will leave me alone.

I always prayed hard, but it didn't seem to make any difference whether Daddy was in a good or bad mood. It didn't matter if he was laughing and joking or ranting and raving when he came in, I never knew what would happen next. Sometimes he got into bed and fell straight into the deep sleep I prayed for, but mostly he didn't.

It started when I was seven years old.

'Cynthia, you're to sleep in the double bed, d'you hear me?' Mammy ordered.

Normally, I slept in the single bed in the same room, but I didn't argue with Mammy. She didn't like it if I argued, and so I always tried hard not to. If I made her cross she hit me round the head or called me horrible names, so I always did as I was told.

When Daddy got into bed he started to tuck himself up right behind me. He was very close, and I didn't like it. I could feel his bare legs against mine and they felt horrible.

This wasn't what I had expected at all – and now what was happening?

Daddy was moving in a strange, shuffling way behind me. I felt frightened of him, petrified whenever I heard his footsteps on the stairs at night. When Daddy started doing other things too, much worse things, I absolutely dreaded going to bed and would lie there every night shaking with nerves and feeling sick with fear.

I never knew what he would do, and even if he did nothing I expected the worst and lay there feeling terrified, especially when he would come in drunk and raging.

'You're a fuckin' whore,' Daddy would shout. 'You're nothing but a stupid bitch.'

I'd squirm under the covers as I heard her scream back at him. She wasn't frightened of him and always gave him the fight he seemed to be looking for.

'You bastard! Don't call me a whore! I bet you're the one who's been sleeping around. Don't you come near me ...'

She would totally lose control of her temper.

'Where's the money? Have you been gambling again, you stupid bastard?'

Mammy looked fiery, with long red hair and blazing green eyes. I'm sure she drank more than Daddy, and she certainly matched him insult for insult.

They never had ordinary conversations and seemed to really hate each other. They tried to avoid each other as much as possible, but whenever they were in the same room they seemed to be fighting and arguing.

'Fuck off, woman!' Daddy would shout as he slapped Mammy across the face or punched her body. 'Leave me alone, you stupid cow.'

Daddy was quite a small man, and he and Mammy looked like an even match for each other in their fights. But she always came off worse. Neither got really badly hurt, they just got madder and madder with each other.

It was like watching a wrestling match that had burst out of the telly and landed in our living room, and it just went on and on as they traded insults and blows.

At nightime I covered my ears when their voices rose through the old lino on the bedroom floor and bounced off the wood-panelled walls around me.

I hated listening to it, but the house was so small that however hard I pressed my hands over my ears, I could never seem to block the noises out.

I would lie in bed picturing exactly what I was hearing.

Mammy would be stalking round in her dirty, floral dress

with her knitted cardigan swinging wildly across her bosom, and Daddy would be swaggering around in the same saggy black trousers he wore every day.

I never really knew how or why the argument started, and I wondered if they did themselves. It seemed that even just the sight of each other made them so angry they wanted to hurt and lash out.

I said lots of prayers to God asking them to stop fighting, but no matter how much I pleaded nothing changed.

Once my father had got into bed with me that first time I prayed even harder for them to stop. I was scared his fights with Mammy might make him act more strangely and hurt me more, but I soon learned that there was no routine at all.

When my prayers *were* answered, it was such a huge relief, because I knew that when Daddy fell asleep, he never stirred again until 7 a.m.

He would get out of bed the minute he woke up and rarely said a word to anyone. Every day he put on his dirty clothes off the floor, smoothed Brylcreem through his greasy black hair, washed his teeth over the kitchen sink using a bar of carbolic soap and the family's one toothbrush, splashed on some Old Spice and stormed off to work.

That was his routine every working day, and I loved hearing the door slam behind him as much as I loved hearing him fall asleep at night.

Even if Daddy left me alone in bed, though, I never slept well. My head itched really badly. It didn't matter how much

I scratched and scratched, the lice kept crawling all over my scalp, driving me mad.

I clawed and dug my fingernails deep into my scalp to make them stop, but that made the itching worse.

My skin crawled too, because all our beds were jumping with fleas. I knew this because if ever we had a visitor, Mammy used special powder to get rid of them, but otherwise she mostly didn't bother.

I could feel them biting me all over as I lay there. I'd try my best not to itch, but when I couldn't stand it any longer I would rake at my skin with my fingernails, making the bites bleed and weep. It felt like a thousand fleas gnawed at me every night, but however deeply I scratched the itching never stopped.

There was no heating in our house either, save for the coal fire in the living room, so in winter the bedroom was freezing cold. All the blankets and sheets smelled terrible and had dirty marks all over them. Some had blood and other nasty stains, but it was so cold I had to use them.

When there weren't enough blankets to go round I put coats on top of me to keep warm. They prickled my skin and smelled of dust and dirt, but the cold was so bad I'd have huddled under anything to stop myself from freezing.

I always slept in just my vest and knickers, or just my knickers. I never owned a pair of pyjamas.

Mammy usually slept in her clothes. She did own a few satin nightgowns, given to her by one of my aunts, but she rarely bothered changing into them. She stayed up all night.

Sometimes she didn't come upstairs until just before 7 a.m., when Daddy got up. It meant they were hardly ever in bed together. Mammy said she had jobs to do downstairs at night like cleaning and washing, but our house was never clean and our clothes were always filthy.

The lino on the floor had a thick layer of dirt on top, the white bits on the patterned wallpaper were stained yellow like Mammy's fingers and the kitchen at the back of the living room was covered in thick grease and grime. Daddy had to shout at Mammy to get her to wash his shirts for work when they got too dirty.

I felt very lonely lying in bed in the dark feeling smelly and dirty and itchy. I always stared into the blackness for hours, only falling asleep when misery and discomfort had sapped my very last drop of energy.

It was pitch black in the bedroom, even in summer, because Mammy insisted we always had a thick black blanket nailed over the window. It was the same with all the front windows in the house. The downstairs was just one room, and the front window looked on to the street, but you could never see out.

Mammy told me it was to keep the sun out, which I thought was a shame, because it meant the house always felt cold and gloomy and suffocating.

Mammy was forever telling us that what happened at home was 'nobody's business but ours'. I wondered if she put the black blankets up because really she didn't want people to look in. 'Don't you go telling anyone what goes on in our house,' she'd warn. 'I don't want anyone poking their nose in our business, do you hear?'

I knew she felt strongly about this, because usually she gave me a clout round the ear to emphasize her point. 'Keep your mouth shut, you little bitch. Don't answer the door. Don't let anyone in, d'you hear me?'

The hall window was the 'strictest' window of all in the house, and Mammy was always going on about it.

'Don't you dare move that blanket, you little cow!' she warned me, time and time again, raising her hand to show me what I would get if I disobeyed her.

Mammy only allowed us to have one lightbulb in the house, and that was usually used in the living room. I hated going to the toilet at night, not just because I was scared of spiders crawling up my ankles outside in the dark, but because I was terrified of picking my way through the pitch-black house and into the backyard to use it.

Mammy would sometimes put extra lightbulbs in if one of her relatives visited, but she took them out as soon as they left. It made me think that it couldn't be right to keep the house in darkness – so why did she do it? Why didn't she want us to see at night?

She told me it was because we couldn't afford lightbulbs, but she said it with an odd look on her face, which made me think it wasn't true. I knew we could afford cigarettes and alcohol, because we always had lots of Mammy's favourite drinks, and she and Daddy smoked sixty cigarettes each a day.

Lightbulbs cost less than cigarettes, didn't they? I didn't think we could be that poor.

The front bedroom of the house was the most stifling room of all, because of the smell from the toilet bucket and the stink of stale smoke and sweat that always hung in the air. Every night I felt as if I was trapped there all alone, even when I wasn't.

There were always other kids in the house. I already had five older siblings when I was born in October 1961, but I always felt like the odd one out, the one who didn't fit in, and was on my own.

My oldest brother, Joe, lived round the corner with Granny, and my three big sisters were much more grown-up than me. Esther was nearly eight years older, Margaret six years older, and Catherine was almost five by the time I was born.

My other brother, Peter, was just two years older than me, but he always acted really grown up and had a reputation for being tough and streetwise. Mammy adored him. I looked up to Peter and wanted him to like me. I felt safe when I was with him, because everybody in the neighbourhood thought he was 'hard'. He seemed to carry this reputation like a badge of honour. It was almost as if, the worse he behaved, the more Mammy protected, loved and cherished him.

With me, she was totally different. She never said a kind word to me or gave me a cuddle, and she regularly started fights and beat me.

'Cynthia, will you empty the bucket now!' she said to me

one day. It was 4.30 p.m. I'd already done the washing-up after school and been to the shop for her cigarettes, while she had just got out of bed after another late night. That was her routine every single day.

'I won't be a minute, Mammy,' I shouted. My stomach turned over at the thought of emptying that toilet bucket, but it was one of the many chores I had to do, or else. Mammy kept an old jam jar by her bed that she'd spit and cough phlegm into, and it would be my job to empty that out too. I loathed it.

Peter was nowhere to be seen, and my big sisters were out, as usual. I felt like the baby stuck at home with Mammy doing the chores and being shouted at, smacked and hit, however hard I worked.

'Get up here now, you lazy bitch,' Mammy screamed again. 'The bucket needs emptying right now!'

I ran upstairs in a panic. She was in a terrible mood, and I didn't want to risk a bad beating, so I grabbed the bucket quickly and headed downstairs.

It was full to the brim, and the smell was diabolical. I retched and stumbled, and suddenly I was falling: I had dropped the bucket and the stinking contents slopped everywhere.

I didn't see her coming at me, but the next thing I felt was the smashing of Mammy's fists into my back. I gasped in shock, breathing in a cloud of vile-smelling air, and retched so badly my stomach felt as if it had jumped up into my throat. When I looked around I felt a stinging 'slap, slap, slap' across my cheeks.

Mammy was looming tall over me, her green eyes flashing crazily and her red hair dancing like flames around her.

'Sorry, Mammy, I'll clean it up quick, Mammy,' I cried.

But there was no stopping her now, and she started to punch me in the stomach and down my arms, then in my face. My head was spinning and I was sure I was going to throw up, what with the smell and the pain.

'You stupid little bitch. Didn't I tell you you're a stupid, lazy little bitch!'

I didn't think I had been lazy. As usual, I'd done the washing-up the minute I got in from school, hoping it would make Mammy less likely to give me a beating. The water was so cold it made my fingers numb. Maybe that's why I dropped the bucket? I really wished I hadn't.

I winced in pain as I tried to clean up the mess with an old rag and more ice-cold water, still trying to work out why Mammy called me lazy. I always worked hard to keep the dishes clean. She left them there all day, waiting for me to come home. How could *I* be lazy when *she* was the one in bed all day?

The washing-up was a tough job. Mammy never bought washing-up liquid or any other cleaning products, and we only ever had one dirty old tea towel, which was never washed. It meant the dishes were never properly clean. It didn't help that when Daddy came home drunk he would often wee in the sink, regardless of whether the dishes were in there or not.

Whatever mess was left for me, I always tried hard to get rid of the smell and wash the dishes as best I could. I mustn't have done it well enough that day. That must be the reason Mammy called me lazy, because I couldn't think of anything else.

Daddy came in unexpectedly that night. He usually went straight to the pub from work, but tonight he'd come home for his tea.

For a second I was pleased to see him. Maybe it was the day he gave Mammy her housekeeping money, which usually made her happy for a while.

But Daddy looked furious and was sucking hard on a cigarette when he came into the sitting room. He spoke to Mammy in an angry voice, and then I felt his beady eyes track me across the room.

'Get here now!' he screamed, pulling his leather belt off his trousers. I froze in fright, and in a flash I was being dragged across the living-room floor, and my bare legs were being whipped and whipped.

'Please, Daddy, no!' I yelped. 'Please stop!' I was already bruised and sore from my mother's beating. The extra pain was unbearable.

He was coughing and choking with the effort of beating me and didn't seem to hear my pleas. The lashings went on and on, with him shouting, 'Fucking bitch! Messy little bitch! I'll teach you. Fuckin' little cow.'

The belt buckle cut into the tender skin on my thighs and smashed across my knuckles when I tried to defend myself.

He left me crying in a crumpled little heap on the cold

floor while he ate his tea, swore at Mammy about the state of his boiled ham and cabbage and went to the pub saying, 'Fuck the lot o' you.'

I couldn't sit down comfortably for days afterwards. I didn't even bother showing Mammy, because I knew she would show no sympathy and wouldn't even offer me a plaster.

I knew she didn't care about me, and that I was her least favourite child. The only time she spoke to me was to order me about, tell me to do the housework or to insult me.

'You're trouble,' she'd tell me. 'You're the awkward one. Get out of my sight. Don't you know, Peter is my favourite? I don't like you, Cynthia! Didn't I tell you that already?' Then she'd cackle like a witch or give me one of her funny false smiles, which scared me.

She regularly told my siblings and relatives I was bad, and seemed to delight in doing so. 'That child is trouble. Don't trust her, she's an evil little bitch. She's a lying little cow. A devil child.'

I didn't know why Mammy said those things, and nobody seemed to argue with her or defend me. I didn't blame them, I was just very confused about why Mammy hated me so much.

I worked hard and listened to what the priests in church and the nuns at school taught me about being a good girl. Living in a strong Catholic community, it was drummed into me all the time that 'bold' girls were sinners, and I knew what happened to sinners: they would burn in hell.

'Be sure your sins will find you out,' Mother Dorothy would say at school. From a young age, I'd tremble in my seat, imagining the flames of hell licking up my legs because I'd forgotten to say my prayers or had missed church on Sunday again.

I didn't cause problems, I tried to avoid them. Yet I always seemed to end up in the most trouble. I couldn't work it out. I'm sure I gave Mammy no reason to hate me.

Sometimes she was nastier to me when she had been drinking a lot. I knew drinking was her favourite pastime, and that other mammies didn't stay in bed all day, but I didn't blame the drinking for the way she treated me, because Mammy always drank. I didn't know any different.

Daddy usually had a reason for beating me, but Mammy seemed to pick arguments out of thin air and turn the whole house upside down in a split-second.

It didn't seem to make any difference what I said or did, she always had it in for me, and twisted everything I said into an argument. She'd smack me round the head all the time, so I was often scared of asking the most basic questions, even when I got older. Throughout my childhood, I thought twice about most things I said, afraid of her reaction.

'Mammy, please can you buy some soap?' I asked once. I picked my moment carefully, while she was looking calm, doing her knitting and listening to Johnny Cash on the radio.

'What do you want soap for?' she shouted, throwing her knitting needles down and clouting me round the ear. 'You're a dirty little bitch, who are you washin' yourself for?'

I had no idea what she was on about, I just wanted soap because I didn't want to be smelly. I didn't understand how I could be called dirty for wanting to clean myself with soap.

Mammy used the word 'dirty' a lot. She also called me a 'filthy whore', and often told me that my private parts were 'filthy' parts of my body. She made a fuss of dressing or undressing in front of me, and if I walked into the bedroom when she was in her bra or nightdress, she shouted: 'What are you looking at, you dirty bastard!'

Of all us kids, everybody said I looked the most like Mammy. People would see me in the local shops and say: 'You've got to be Josie Murphy's daughter – you're the image of her!'

Later on, I would wonder if, for some strange reason, that was why she hated me so much. Did I look too much like her, despite my blond hair? Was that why she had it in for me? It didn't make sense, but there had to be some reason.

I remember unsuspecting relatives and neighbours often used to say, 'Poor Josie, she's got her work cut out!' They seemed to feel sorry for Mammy because she had lots of kids and not much money.

I didn't really understand why they said she had her work cut out though, she barely did any work at all. I think they thought she was stuck in the house, working her fingers to the bone, but I knew that wasn't true.

Daddy worked really hard though, and he seemed to be well respected too. Even though he was always dressed in shabby old clothes, he still made a good impression, like you couldn't ignore him when he walked into a room. He didn't scare me as much as Mammy, but I was still afraid of his temper, and I always tried not to make him angry.

He drank for hours every single night, but he didn't get drunk as often as Mammy. And at least he worked; even at weekends he did extra jobs to get more money. He always put food on the table, as well as plenty of cigarettes and alcohol for Mammy, and in return he spent every night in his favourite pub lounges at the Club, McDonagh's, Hogan's, the Arches or the Queens in Dalkey. Mammy didn't complain. I think she was glad to have him out of her sight.

Daddy was employed by the local Dun Laoghaire Corporation all his working life, first as a street cleaner and then as the clerk of the town hall. He wasn't particularly badly paid, but we went without lots of things because he and Mammy chose to spend nearly all of the money on drink and cigarettes.

Daddy's job seemed to give him some recognition in the community. Everybody knew him and seemed to like him, and they treated him like a big man.

'Give my regards to your da!' shopkeepers would call out as I walked by. 'How's your Daddy doin'? Tell him to call round and see me soon. I'll see him for a pint in Hogans!'

Daddy used to regularly come home with things he had been given, and at Christmas we got huge joints of ham, a giant turkey, bags of coal, yet more cigarettes and cases of beer, sherry, port and whiskey, all from Daddy's friends.

When she'd had a few drinks, Mammy loved to reminisce

and tell colourful tales about the past and her courting days with Daddy.

I lapped up every word when I heard her describe how she used to dance the night away wearing glamorous dresses in the local dance halls, with Daddy swinging on her arm.

She said plenty of other things too – some I didn't understand at the time, and some that turned out to be lies.

Over the years, I've pieced together the truth about my parents' history. My mother was born in 1933 and christened Josephine, but everyone called her Josie.

She grew up with my Granny Mary O'Neill, three sisters, Ann, Mag and Cathleen, and a brother, Henry. Her dad died when she was seven.

She had my oldest brother, Joe, when she was seventeen, but she wasn't thrown into an unmarried mothers' home in disgrace, as young Catholic girls often were in those days.

Instead, she stayed at home with baby Joe, and Granny made quite a fuss of her, from what I hear. Mammy eventually got a job as a housekeeper for a rich family, which meant she was earning quite a bit of money to help pay her keep.

It wasn't long before she was out drinking and dancing again, and she met my father on a night out in Dalkey.

They married when my mother was pregnant with my sister Esther in 1953, and she spent her 'honeymoon' in Holles Street Hospital giving birth.

My father, Peter Murphy, was six years older than my mother, born in 1927. Unlike her, he never once reminisced or even made the slightest reference to his past. As a child, all I knew was that he grew up in an orphanage with his two brothers and four sisters, but he never mentioned any of them, ever.

'Tell me, Daddy, have I got cousins on your side of the family? I'd love to meet them – can't you tell me where they are?'

His reaction was the same every time. 'Will you shut up asking? I can't remember. The past is in the past and leave it at that.'

He wouldn't even tell me what date he was born, so it felt as if he had no past or history behind him, and as soon as a day was over in his life he never spoke about it again. Sometimes I wondered if he'd been dropped off at our house by aliens.

Now I know he was placed in a Catholic orphanage from the age of two and a half, along with his siblings, after my grandmother died. My mother once said my father was sexually abused in the orphanage, but he refused ever to talk about it.

Little wonder my father never discussed his family background.

Chapter 2

Don't Wake Mammy

I'm sitting in the big blue cot in the front bedroom. Peter is wedged up next to me, and we're both sucking on a bottle. It's one of those banana-shaped bottles with teats on both ends, and we're both sucking away like mad, trying to get more milk than the other. The milk tastes sweet, and we can't get enough of it. We're glugging away like demons, pulling silly faces at each other and making slurping sounds. When the milk has all gone we suck air for a while, making funny squeaking noises, and then everything goes very quiet.

We sit with our legs dangling through the bars of the cot, wondering what to do next. My tummy feels warm under my jumper, but my bare feet are stinging with the cold. I'm nearly four years old, and Peter is six.

The room is dark, even though we can hear the birds singing in the morning sky outside. The grey curtains are shut, and behind them the black blanket is firmly nailed in place. Mammy likes to sleep in the daytime while everybody else is out, and we know not to disturb her.

I peep over at her, lying in her double bed next to the cot. Her hair is splayed all over the pillow. I think it looks like golden threads, and I'd like to touch it, but I'm not allowed to touch Mammy. Even when she's awake she doesn't like me to touch her. I wonder what it would be like to hold her hand or sit on her knee. I'd like to try it, but I know she doesn't want me to, because she always shouts something nasty or shoves me away if I get too close.

Her skin looks lily-white against the darkness of the room, and I think she looks pretty, like a lady on the telly, although she isn't in a fancy bed. She's lying on her side, with a brown overcoat piled on top of the covers. The sheets and blankets have hundreds of little holes in them and look very old. Some of them have blood on them. Mammy doesn't seem to mind though. I never see her wash or change them.

The room smells horrible, as usual, much worse than our outside toilet. My jumper has the same smell, and so does the blanket in the cot and all the dirty clothes on the floor. Even my dolly's hair has a stinky smell, and sometimes I can't get to sleep because of the stench that hangs in the air after Daddy uses the bucket late at night.

There is a glass dish next to Mammy's bed that's piled high with ash and the end bits of cigarettes, and I can still smell the smoke from last night. It mustn't smell that bad to Mammy though, because she never empties the bucket or the ashtray, even when they are full, and she always sleeps very deeply, like nothing bothers her at all.

I stare at her face. Some days her cheeks are red and puffy, but Mammy always puts bright-red lipstick on at night to sit in the chair and have a drink, or to do her knitting while she listens to country and western music or watches the news. This morning she's still wearing her lipstick. It's a little bit smudged, like the way it looked when I put it on my dolly once, but there are no sores spoiling Mammy's face today, so that's good.

There was a fight downstairs last night.

This one began like lots of others, when Daddy came in from the pub. It was very late when I heard his key in the lock, but I was still wide awake. I couldn't sleep because my head was really itchy, and I couldn't stop scratching it.

I felt scared when I heard the front door creak open, wondering what would happen. I held my breath, listening to see if Mammy and Daddy would start shouting or hitting each other.

'You're a selfish bastard!' Mammy yelled, and my heart went cold. 'You're a good-for-nothing lazy bastard!'

I heard her race across the room into the hallway and hit Daddy lots of times with her fists. I think he slapped her across the face, because I recognized the sound it made from when Mammy slapped my face. 'Fuck off, you mad whore!' Daddy yelled. 'Get away from me, you madwoman. Go back to your sherry.'

I didn't want to hear any more. It made me so sad and afraid, and I wanted it all to stop for ever. Even though Mammy isn't ever kind to me, and Daddy doesn't seem to notice me, I want them to be happy. Then maybe I will be happy too.

I buried my head deep under my blanket, held my hands tightly over my ears and said a little prayer. 'Please God, can you make everything nice and quiet? Amen.'

I think He might have heard me, because when I woke up, Daddy had already gone to work, and Mammy was fast asleep under the coat.

Now the house is ever so quiet. All I can hear is the birds and the rustling of trees in the breeze outside the window, and Mammy breathing deeply.

When I hear the rag-and-bone man outside, shouting, 'Any old rags! Any old rags!' I climb out of the cot and peep through a tiny crack in the side of the blanket on the window to catch a glimpse, making sure I don't let too much light in and wake Mammy.

I scuttle around quietly in my bare feet, knowing full well that if I make any noise or knock one of Mammy's holy statues off the sideboard by mistake there will be big trouble.

I watch the rag-and-bone man for ages, longing to run down the street after him. I see him give a little girl a bright-yellow balloon and wish I could have one too. Mammy won't let me open the front door or go out on my own.

Sometimes we didn't have enough money to pay the rent or the milkman, so Mammy never let any of us kids open the door, in case it was someone 'knockin' for money we don't have'.

Even when I was allowed to play in the street with the older ones, all of us had to use the back door.

Today, I can see other little ones out for a stroll with their mammies, but my mammy never takes me anywhere. A neighbour goes by. She has lots of little kids but still looks like a teenager, she's so fashionable in her patterned mini skirt with her hair all piled up. She's holding hands with two of her children as they walk to the shops, all of them chattering and laughing.

Mammy doesn't like her. 'Look at her – she looks like an ol' whore! A prostitute!' she said the first time she ever clapped eyes on her. 'No married woman should dress like that!'

I wondered why Mammy said that and what it all meant. The neighbour was a very nice mammy. I wished my mammy would get herself washed and dress up in nice clothes. I wished she would take me for a walk with her hair all done and talk to me and make me laugh, but she never once did. My mammy wore dirty dresses with cigarette ash spilled down the front, and she hardly ever left the house.

We had a television downstairs, but if anybody asked what was on, the answer was usually 'on the bloody blink'. I wasn't allowed to touch anything like that while Mammy slept. Sometimes Peter and I made up games with a couple of dolls that had been scribbled on with biro, or some old wooden blocks. We made the dollies whack and kick each other to pass the time.

It was always cold in the house in the daytime, because the fire was never lit until Mammy got up. My bare feet stung every time they hit the ice-cold lino, and you could see your breath in front of you on winter days.

Sometimes I would root out some old clothes from under the stairs. There were always loads of bags of stuff. Daddy brought them home after there had been a jumble sale at the town hall, and seeing as we didn't have wardrobes, it all stayed in big piles in cupboards.

I'd pretend it was a treasure chest, trying on old belts with shiny buckles and cotton dresses with fancy buttons. Everything smelled of dust and made me sneeze. Nothing looked like it went together, some things had stains on and smelled sweaty and musty like my Granny's long skirts, but it was something to do, and much better than being cold.

At lunchtime, Esther came home. 'Peter, Cynthia, come on and get your dinner!' she shouts, daylight flooding in behind her. Her arrival was the highlight of my day. Esther was kind, and I loved her to bits. Sometimes it felt as if Esther was actually our mammy, because she looked after us so much when Mammy was in bed.

She came home every lunchtime on schooldays and at weekends to fetch us bread and cold meat and give us a drink of milk or water. We never went hungry, although usually there was only just enough to go round and you had to be quick to get your fair share.

Peter and I tucked in like a pair of demons, tearing at the warm bread and gobbling up the scraps of corned beef greedily, stuffing it into our mouths with our dirty fingers.

It was an extra treat if we got to go round the corner to Granny's, because she gave us fruit too. She was great at getting fruit. Some days I went with her to the grocer's at closing time to ask for 'spoilt' fruit and then Granny would chop off the bruised bits and we'd gobble up the guts of a plum or a pear.

Granny was a great storyteller too. 'Come here and sit with me, Cynthia,' she would smile. 'Did I tell you the story about the banshee?' Mammy and Daddy hardly spoke to me at all, let alone told me stories that made my eyes widen like saucers.

I'd sit on the floor beside Granny's long skirts for ages listening to her tales. I loved the one about the banshee, who was an old woman with long white hair who came to warn you of death. Granny told me it again and again, but it was one of my favourites and I lapped it up every time.

'If the banshee howls three times before midnight, then someone in the house will die,' Granny would say with a glint in her eye. 'If you happen to come across her yourself, usually sitting on a wall, combing her long white hair, and she throws her comb at you, then you will die instantly!'

I loved my granny. I heard people say she looked pious, but

I wasn't sure what that meant. She looked like a jolly nun to me, with her round face, big red cheeks and shoulder-length grey hair, which was so straight it looked like it had been ironed. She was sweet and kind, and always made me feel special.

'Be good now, you two,' Esther smiles after lunch when she leaves us at home again, Mammy still in bed. 'I'll be back as soon as you know it.'

Every time I watch my big sister disappear round the corner of our street, my heart aches for her to come back.

Often I sit on the greasy lino under the kitchen table, scratching the bites on my legs. Sometimes I scratch so much I make myself bleed, and then yellow stuff bubbles up on my skin, so I wipe it away with the squares of old newspaper we use as toilet paper.

I scratch my head too. I can feel things crawling in my hair. I try to pick out whatever it is, but I can never tell if I catch anything because my fingernails are black. I don't think I do, because the itching just gets worse and worse the more I pick.

It seems like I spend hours some days, just sitting there doing nothing, waiting for the bigger ones to get home, wondering how long they will be.

When they do come home, Mammy gets out of bed and lights the fire.

I like the warmth and I like the bustle when the house first starts to fill up, but on some days it feels like living in a big cooking pot. With so many of us around, I sometimes feel hot and bothered, like something is going to boil over at any minute.

One day it does. Mammy suddenly yells something out so loudly it makes my ears whistle. She sounds livid, as if she wants to kill someone. 'Who did that? How dare you!' Now she is hitting me with a sweeping brush, bashing it into my back. I have no idea what has caused this particular outburst, but I have no choice but to endure it.

I shut my eyes as tightly as I can, so tight my whole face aches. I can hear my howls and screams echoing round my head, and my bones are rattling inside my body.

I keep my eyes glued together and huddle myself into a ball. I make myself as small as possible as Mammy moves away from my cowering body. I just want to be invisible, so nobody will notice me and I won't get another beating for getting in the way.

When Mammy's voice gets near to me again, I hug my knees in closer to my chest, pulling my skirt down to make a tent over my ankles and pushing my forehead into my kneecaps.

Amongst the shouting and screaming I hear the front door open and shut, and I freeze when I hear my oldest brother Joe's voice. 'Jesus, what's up with you?' he says.

Joe only ever comes round at night when Daddy is in the pub. He lives with my Granny, so I'm not used to him being around much.

I always pray Daddy won't come in when Joe is there, as any change in routine can set Daddy off on a rant. It doesn't take much. Any one of us can be the cause of a fight. Drink makes it all much worse. He will explode with anger and start telling anyone, but especially Joe, to 'Fuck off out of here'.

Mammy will defend her oldest son and start fighting with Daddy. Sometimes, I sit hugging my knees for hours, praying for calm. My mind often clouds over, and I try to think about nice things. Maybe I'll be allowed to go to school with my big sisters soon? Nobody ever talks to me about school, but I imagine it to be some magical place, like stepping into a whole new shiny world of friends and books and fun.

I don't think my dream will come true any time soon. I never dare hope that good things might happen to me, ever. Peter is two years older than me, and he doesn't go to school, so I think I have a long time to wait until I can be a big girl, instead of being stuck in the cold, dark house all day.

But, a few weeks later, Mammy said she had something to tell me. I was surprised because she hardly ever spoke to me or told me anything.

'Now, Cynthia, you're going to be starting school tomorrow with your brother,' she announced, no warmth in her voice at all.

I couldn't believe what I was hearing and was worried that Mammy was telling me lies, but she said Peter and I were to join the baby class together, on the very same day!

'You're jokin' me, Mammy, aren't you? Is it true, is it really true? How come we're starting together?'

Mammy told me Peter couldn't start school until he came off the bottle, and now he was six he was old enough to give up his milk. 'Aren't you the lucky ones, starting together? It'll keep the two of you out of trouble,' she said.

Mammy had another baby by now, my little sister, Mary. I was no longer the baby of the family, and I was starting school. I felt incredibly grown up. I was thrilled to be joining my three big sisters, and delighted my big brother would be in the very same class as me.

Best of all, I didn't have to stay stuck in the house any more. I hated it. Even having a new baby sister hadn't made it any more of a home. I loved babies, and Mary was adorable, but she cried a lot and Mammy seemed more tired than ever, because she even slept when Mary was screaming.

I did my best to help Mammy get the milk and change the cloths she used for nappies, because that's what the older kids were expected to do in our house, but school would be much more fun.

I imagined myself surrounded by hundreds of storybooks and mountains of pens and paper, devouring every word the nuns said to me. That's what happened at school, wasn't it? I was sure it would be much better than being at home.

I'd never been shown a book before. I'd been told that Mammy couldn't read or write, and we had no books in the house. Daddy read the newspapers, and I often looked at the pictures, but he never read anything out to me. Now I was going to learn to read like a big girl, and I couldn't wait to get started.

I'd make friends too! And not just with the kids who lived in the council houses by us who I saw in the street and the shops sometimes. I'd make friends from all over Dalkey – with kids from the fancy big houses up by the beach and the mansions around Dalkey Hill and Killiney Hill, where Esther sometimes took me for a walk or a picnic.

The night before I started, I picked up a few things about the school from my sisters. I heard it had a great reputation and lots of parents fought over places. We only lived a ten minute walk away, so all the Murphy kids got a place without a fight.

I wanted to make a fine first impression. There was no uniform, so I went rummaging under the stairs.

As well as the clothes Daddy brought home from the jumble sales, there were bags of clothes kind people had left on the doorstep, knowing there were lots of kids to clothe in our house, as well as some navy-blue school knickers donated by the St Vincent de Paul charity.

I was thrilled beyond words when Esther helped me get dressed for my first day. I had a navy skirt I didn't remember any of my sisters ever wearing, so that was officially mine. I added a long-sleeved shirt, and an old V-neck jumper of Peter's, I rolled the sleeves up because they were too long. It wasn't perfect, as girls were meant to wear roundnecks, but I was happy with it all the same.

All I needed was shoes. The only ones that looked the part and more or less fitted had broken buckles, but Mammy told me not to wear them in any case, because I didn't have any socks. Instead, I finished off my outfit with a pair of blue Wellingtons, and we were off!

Esther walked me and Peter to school on our first morning. I looked at the other kids, all with their mammies, and wished my mammy could walk with me to school too. But I knew she was still in bed. She never walked any of her kids to school or even got up to wave us off.

It didn't matter. I was beside myself at the thought of meeting the holy nuns who would teach us, imagining them to be very wise and kind old ladies who would fill my head with fascinating facts and amazing stories like the ones Granny told me.

I'd seen nuns at church, even though we hardly ever went. Daddy would go to funerals or First Holy Communions, which were always very big occasions in our village, but Mammy didn't like going to church at all. She had pictures of the Pope and Jesus hanging on the walls, holy ornaments on the fireplace, and once there was even a pot of holy water we had to dip our fingers in on the way into the bedroom.

But Mammy told us only sinners went to church, to ask God for forgiveness. 'We're better off at home,' she'd say. 'I'm not going again and havin' posh folk lookin' down their noses at us!'

Sometimes the parish priest would come hammering on our door of a Sunday evening, demanding to know why we hadn't been in church again. Daddy would go mad about being 'shamed' on his own doorstep like that.

Mammy would stub out her cigarette and rush to the door to tell the priest one of us kids had been 'so very ill, Father' even when I was sure everyone was well. I thought it wasn't right to tell a fib to the priest, but I knew better than to say anything.

The following Sunday an older sibling would have to take us to church to 'shut the priest up' and 'stop him sticking his nose in where it's not wanted'.

On the rare occasion I did go to church, I liked the feeling of peace there. Nobody shouted, and I knew nobody was going to hit me, what with the good priest and holy nuns all around. I believed in God and said lots of prayers. I felt safe, and it was nice and clean and bright compared to our house.

I was sure being taught by nuns in a grand school was going to be just like going to church, only better. I simply couldn't wait to start, and I grinned all the way there on my first day.

Chapter 3

Meeting Mr Greeny

The school stood like a giant palace by the sea. The blue water was twinkling behind it, and it looked so grand it took my breath away. Although I was only four-years-old, the closer I got to the towering building, the tinier I felt.

By the time I walked through the doors I felt as small as one of the grains of sand on the beach, and butterflies started to flutter in my tummy.

It was busy and noisy in the wide hallway, and I was relieved when Peter and I were ushered into a classroom. It felt safer in there, even though there were lots of children filing in around us. The sound of shoes on wood echoed around me, and I saw that there were row upon row of wooden desks. They seemed to go on for ever, and were raised on steps the further back you looked.

I squeezed Peter's hand and tucked myself into his side.

'My name is Mrs O'Reilly,' said an old lady with fluffy white hair, clapping her hands sharply to make us all look round. She was standing by a big blackboard at the front of the class and looked stern. I felt scared.

'Boys are to sit on one side, girls on the other,' she said firmly. My bottom lip started to wobble when Peter pulled away from me. I felt lost and so alone, and hot tears burst from my eyes.

'What is it, child?" asked Mrs O'Reilly. 'Can you not be seated like all the other children?'

'Please, Miss, I don't want to be parted from my brother,' I sobbed.

Forty pairs of curious eyes turned to me. I felt so silly and small, and I just wanted to disappear.

'Very well,' said Mrs O'Reilly briskly. 'Just for today, we can make an exception – but just this once, young lady. There'll be no more of this.'

I sat down quietly next to Peter on the boy's side, but I could tell I was still being watched. Stealing a glance up through my wet eyes, I saw a wobbly sea of rosy pink cheeks, smart new jumpers, crisp cotton dresses and neat new haircuts.

The girls had pretty hairclips and dazzling white socks. The boys looked as if they'd been scrubbed from head to toe ten times over. Their faces shone, their clothes were beautifully clean and creased in all the right places, and their hair was freshly clipped.

I shuffled uncomfortably in my seat and stared down at a deep line of ink etched along a groove in the wood of my desk. Why were they staring at me so hard? I glanced at my navy skirt. There were little bobbles on the front, so it didn't look brand-new like the other girls' skirts and dresses. I had dirty rings around my cuffs too. But I wasn't scruffy. I looked fine, didn't I?

Sometimes Mammy filled up the tin bath and put it in front of the fire on a Sunday night so all us kids could have a wash. I frowned when I thought about it, because I couldn't for the life of me remember the last time I'd been in it.

I wished I'd had a bath last night so that I would look all scrubbed up like the other children. Maybe they wouldn't be staring then, maybe they would be smiling and trying to be friendly instead?

I didn't like the bath. I shuddered when I thought about how the water was always cold and gave me goosebumps. We had no soap, and the whole family shared one towel. I usually went in last, when the water had a film of greasy dirt on top, so I guess I never looked all scrubbed up anyway. The bath wouldn't have made a difference. No, it didn't matter that I hadn't had a bath. I didn't remember Daddy ever having a bath, and lots of people liked him. He had lots of friends. I was going to be fine.

The eyes kept watching me, making me wriggle and fidget. Maybe they were just curious because I cried and I was sitting on the boy's side? I squinted around again, feeling confused and trying to work out why I felt so out of place. My heart started to sink when I worked out that my hair must look very messy indeed compared to the other girls'. I scratched it all the time, and I didn't have a brush, so I just knew it was sticking out in all directions like it always did.

I felt so embarrassed that I wished I could turn invisible, but instead it felt as if every light hanging from the ceiling and every pair of eyes was shining on me, making me stand out even more.

I glanced at my hands, and seeing a thick ridge of dirt under each of my fingernails, I quickly sat on them to hide them. Next I tucked my feet as far behind me as I could, to hide my Wellingtons under my chair. Nobody else had Wellingtons on, it seemed like they all had shiny new shoes.

Mrs O'Reilly told me I could choose where I wanted to sit over on the girl's side. I scoured the room nervously, and my gaze fell on a girl I recognized from going to the shops near our house. She wasn't staring at me like the others, and I noticed her clothes didn't look as fancy, so I asked if I could sit by her. She gave me a friendly smile, and from that day on we became good friends.

Later, we were told an older girl was coming into the class to help out, as Mrs O'Reilly had to leave early, and to my delight it turned out to be Esther. That put a big smile on my face, even though I sensed from that very first day that school was not going to be the wonderful place I had dreamed of.

When the neighbours and local shopkeepers asked me how school was I said, 'Grand.' In some ways, it was. The bits I liked were that it was warm and clean and I didn't have to worry about what Mammy might do, but I didn't say that to anybody. That's what I thought of school though. Despite the fact that I hadn't settled in yet, I reckoned it was going to be far better than being at home.

I can clearly remember meeting Mother Dorothy, who ran the school. She was very tall and looked fierce and strict. She made us quake just by walking in the room, and we all sat to attention and watched and listened in perfect silence, lined up like little soldiers, hanging on her every word.

With a stony face, she told us that bold behaviour would not be tolerated. God was everywhere, watching our every move. As she said this, she looked straight at me, and I felt very uncomfortable, but I didn't know why. I was sure I hadn't done anything wrong, but by the way she looked at me, Mother Dorothy seemed to think I had.

We were to be sure our sins would be found out, Mother Dorothy went on. If we sinned, we would have to do penance. I thought that must mean saying the Hail Mary and asking God to pray for us, like I did at church. I liked saying my prayers, so that was fine.

But then Mother Dorothy said that if we didn't do enough penance we would go to the burning fires of hell! How much penance was enough? How many prayers would I have to say to stop being burned? I had no idea at all, but I made a secret vow to say extra prayers that night, just to be safe.

'Make no mistake,' she continued, pointing a bony finger around the class, 'I will see to it that bold children are severely punished. They will be punished in front of the whole class!' As she said this, she banged a long, thin cane into the wooden floor, which made such a loud noise we all sat up even more.

Now I was rigid with fear, my spine straighter than the cane as I sat bolt upright. Being punished in front of the whole class sounded worse than going to the burning fires of hell. Ever since that first day, all I had wanted was to hide at the back of the class so nobody could see my scruffy clothes and messy hair, and I was terrified of being beaten with a cane in front of all these other children.

I could tell from the start Mother Dorothy didn't like me. I watched her smile at other children all the time, asking politely after their parents. 'I saw your daddy on television last night,' I'd hear her say to one of the rich kids. 'What wonderful work he's doing! Please send him my regards. Has your mother got a new car? How lovely!'

But she seemed only ever to scowl at me, and before long she was giving out steam to me all the time.

'You stupid child! What are you wearing? You'll catch pneumonia!' she barked one day. I didn't have a coat, it was lashing down with rain, and Mammy had ordered me to wear a pair of old sandals with no socks instead of my Wellington boots. I didn't know why, but I didn't argue. Sometimes Mammy made up funny rules like that. If I argued I knew Mammy would go mad and hit me, so I did as I was told.

My toes felt like little icicles, and I was frozen to the bone, but I didn't think Mother Dorothy really cared about how I felt, because every time she spoke to me she always made me feel worse. 'I'm real sorry, Reverend Mother, truly I am,' I said, pleading for forgiveness with my eyes and not knowing what else to say.

Mammy didn't like me telling anyone our business, so I couldn't say I didn't have any socks or shoes at home. 'I promise faithfully I won't do it again,' I said, not knowing if Mammy would let me wear the Wellingtons the next day or not.

'Make quite sure you don't, you stupid girl,' said Mother Dorothy. 'Or you will have me to answer to.'

However much I tried to be invisible, she always found a reason to pick on me, and her criticisms just got worse.

I knew whenever she was gunning for me. Her dark eyes would narrow as she lowered her forehead and directed her steely glare straight between my eyes. I always started to quiver like a little leaf, knowing I was in for another shameful telling-off.

'Cynthia Murphy, come to the front of the class now!' she demanded one day.

Cheeks glowing bright red, I trooped up and stood there, squirming inside, wondering what I had done this time. I wanted the ground to swallow me up, and I felt like bolting for the door, but I stood rooted to the spot, burning with shame, as everybody stared at me once more.

'Why are you wearing that filthy jumper again? I told you last time to smarten yourself up, young lady. Look at your hair! Have you never brushed it? Class, will you look at this dirty girl? What a terrible child!'

I was absolutely devastated every time she picked on me. I wanted to learn, not be told off. Mammy and Daddy didn't have enough money to buy me new clothes to make me look smart like the other children. It wasn't my fault, and it wasn't fair.

It didn't take long before I started to feel cross with Mother Dorothy. There was nothing I could do about the way I looked. Mammy was always telling me how very poor we were. That's why wealthier people from the neighbourhood left charity bags on our doorstep. I picked out the nicest things I could from under the stairs, but they were never good enough. I didn't have shampoo or a hairbrush, so I couldn't wash or brush my hair, and we never had any toothpaste or a flannel, so I couldn't help having dirty teeth and a grubby face.

One day, instead of calling out my name, Mother Dorothy marched over to my desk, grabbed hold of my shoulders and pulled me violently out of my chair.

I gasped in shock, and my brain started whirling as I tried to work out what I had done wrong. It must be something really bad, because she looked madder than ever before.

I'd been at school a few years by now, and Mother Dorothy had started to tell me off for not having the copy books and pencils Mammy and Daddy were meant to provide, and for not doing my homework.

I couldn't tell her that Mammy wouldn't give me any money for those things, or that she refused to let me do my homework. I was sure Mother Dorothy would think I was lying and would tell me nobody's mammy behaved like that. But mine did. 'Education is a waste of time – you're a girl,' Mammy said whenever I asked for a pencil or a book. 'You'll just get married and have babies, what's the point in learnin'?

'Peel the potatoes instead,' she'd tell me. 'Make the beds, clean the gas cooker for your mammy.' I didn't even have a school bag to carry my work in. How could I tell Mother Dorothy all that? I just couldn't. What if she went knocking on our door? Daddy always threatened me with trouble if the nuns came complaining, and he would probably beat me with his leather belt for telling people our business.

I had worked out by now that Daddy only liked people to see him as the man he was outside of our house. The side everybody saw was the hardworking family man who grafted by day to feed his kids and enjoyed a drink with all his pals at night. I don't think anybody knew what I did. Nobody knew I lay in bed at night feeling terrified of his fights and rows with Mammy. I was sure no one knew he hardly had anything to do with his family, unless he was shouting or swearing.

All these thoughts crashed around in my head as I let Mother Dorothy drag me to the front of the class, sinking her sharp fingernails into my shoulders as she did so.

I chewed my lip so as not to cry as I waited for her to tell me what I had done that was so very wrong. I knew there was a big list to choose from, because she'd gone though it so many times before. But I wasn't prepared for what she said this time, because it was just so unexpectedly cruel.

'Look, everyone! Cynthia Murphy has lice in her hair!' she said in a nasty, mocking voice. I gasped in shock. I knew I had lice, I always did, but she sounded more like a playground bully than Mother Dorothy.

My heart thumped in my chest. I knew it was wrong, but I couldn't help the thought that flashed though my head: 'You wicked old cow! I'll get you back one day!' I told myself. In that moment, I didn't care if my sinful thoughts would make me burn in hell, as long as I got some revenge on Mother Dorothy.

'Why have you come to school with lice in your hair, child?' she went on, poking me in the shoulder and glaring at me. 'Don't you dare come to school with lice in your hair again, you filthy child. This time it will be ten lashes. Next time I will double it.'

I started to shake uncontrollably when she reached for her green cane. She normally kept 'Mr Greeny', as we called it, locked in a cupboard. This was the first time she had punished me with it.

She had warned that she would bring it out for 'very bad children', and so I knew once and for all that in her eyes I was one of those very bad children. I was sure none of my sins was my fault, but that didn't seem to matter. Mr Greeny and I got to know each other very well over the years to come.

'Hold your hand out,' snapped Mother Dorothy. 'And hold the other hand underneath to keep the top one steady, child! If you move your hand away I will add ten more lashes.'

I held my breath as I held out my hands. I was trembling so much I struggled to keep steady as she had ordered, and the more I shook the more angry Mother Dorothy became.

I recoiled in shock when I stole a glance at her. She was purple with rage and was actually frothing at the mouth as she towered over me with the cane raised high.

I shut my eyes and bit through my lip as the poker-hot pain shot from the palm of my hand and through every vein and nerve in my body.

Everything jangled inside me, and my whole arm felt numb.

'Hold your hand out again, child. Do it now!'

I tried really hard to lift my shaking arm and hold my hand out flat, but the mixture of pain and fear racing round my body made me pull it away the next time Mother Dorothy brought the cane down.

Now she was raging at me even more, shouting and screaming and showering me with froth from her mouth. 'I do not tolerate sinners! Have you no respect? Have you no fear of God?'

It felt like I stood there for hours as Mother Dorothy ranted at me again and again to hold my hand out, but each time she brought the cane down I instinctively pulled away.

'Twenty lashes!' she screamed. 'Thirty lashes! Forty lashes!' but I still couldn't hold my hand out straight. Even through the pain and shame I could tell this wasn't going well for Mother Dorothy. I could hear other children letting out gasps and whispers as they sat glued to the awful spectacle.

Eventually Mother Dorothy threw me outside the classroom and told me she would deal with me later. 'There will be severe consequences,' she warned, which I learned meant being called more bad things like 'evil child' and 'wicked little madam', receiving several sharp slaps across the face, or being marched back down to one of the lower classes so I felt ashamed in front of the younger kids.

Some of my classmates thought I had deliberately defied Mother Dorothy, forcing her to count up in tens until she got to a hundred and looked like she would explode. It happened time and time again, and afterwards they always told me I was really brave.

I did develop a bold and rebellious streak as the years went by. But the truth was I felt terrified of being hit and I couldn't bear the terrible pain it caused. 'You're wrong, I'm a coward,' I told them, but they didn't believe me.

After that very first caning I ran home from school in tears at the end of the day and told Mammy how horrible Mother Dorothy was. I wanted Mammy to see the angry red line across my palm which was still hot and smarting, but she barely looked at me.

'You must have done something terrible to make a holy

nun so mad at you,' was all she said, giving me a clip round the ear. I stumbled towards the bedroom door feeling shocked and dazed. 'Don't leave empty-handed!' my mother called after me from her bed. 'Take my dirty cup downstairs with you, you lazy bitch!'

I tried to tell Daddy too, but he didn't seem to want to listen either. 'You must have deserved it! Why can't you behave yerself? If those nuns come knocking on this door I'll beat you myself and you'll have even more to whinge about!'

I stopped telling them about school after that, and they never asked me anything. They didn't go to any parents' meetings or open days like other mammies and daddies, so I guessed they had no interest in what I was learning or doing all day.

Anyway, they had another baby now, so my school was the last thing they'd care about. My little brother, Martin, was born when I was nearly six-years-old and Mary was just two. He was Mammy's eighth child and, like Mary, he was a beautiful baby.

I worried about how we would cope with another child in the house. I could see how we struggled already, and I feared a new baby would only make matters worse, causing more fights and arguments. It meant that, despite the treatment I was getting from Mother Dorothy, I still preferred to be at school than at home.

I liked the smell of chalk dust, pencil shavings and freshly cut paper, and I was relieved to get away from the smell of stale cigarettes and dirty toilets that hung around at home.

I loved the quiet time best of all, when the teachers ordered us to sit in silence and read a book. Other kids groaned, because they found it boring, but even when I couldn't read a word on the page I lapped up the chance to have some unbroken peace.

At home I never knew when a fight or an argument would break out, but in those reading times at school we always had at least ten minutes to ourselves, and I absolutely loved it.

Mammy told me I had to come home to eat at lunchtime. 'People will be talking about what you're are eating. I don't want people talking,' she said, but I worked out that the real reason was that she didn't want the bother of making pack-up lunches. Instead, whichever kids were around picked up the bread and meat on the way home and shared it out.

Sometimes, when I was a bit older, I was allowed to go to Granny's. I loved those lunchtimes. Granny gave me a smile and a cuddle as I stepped inside, then fed me sandwiches and warm, sweet tea. I didn't mind that her house was even dirtier and colder than ours. I sat on the mucky floor lapping up Granny's tales about the Black and Tans or the Easter Rising, and basking in the warmth of her kindness.

I always wished I could stay longer at Granny's, and I often walked back to school with a lump in my throat, wondering what the nuns might do to me next. I was so scared of Mother Dorothy that on many days it didn't feel much better going to school than having to stay at home.

Quite often, Mammy kept me home from school when,

say, the electric man was coming for his money. She didn't want to have to get dressed and come downstairs to answer the door herself, so she kept me at home to do it for her. The older I got, the more she did it. I found it strange, as it wasn't like we had loads of people coming round to pay us visits.

I hated being stuck in the house. It reminded me of the long, cold days before I started school. I didn't really like being anywhere much. At least the classroom was warmer and brighter, and there were plenty of things to do and learn, but school certainly wasn't the refuge I'd hoped it would be.

Peter wasn't in my class for very long at all, but the good thing was that all the other kids knew I had a big brother in the school who would stand up for me if they bullied me. I think it worked, because most of the time the other kids left me alone.

I had my own friends now too, who came from big families like me. They also got picked on by Mother Dorothy some-times, so we stuck together and looked out for each other. One of my best friends was Eileen. We poked fun at the nuns behind their backs, copying how they walked and talked and collapsing in fits of giggles. The posh kids sometimes said nasty things to me, like: 'I'm not sitting by you, you stink!,' but after a while it didn't even make me flinch. I had my friends, and I was used to Mother Dorothy saying much worse things.

I remember making Eileen laugh with a silly impression at the back of the classroom when Mother Dorothy marched in with a face like thunder.

'What's that smell?' she bellowed, pointing her long nose high into the air and taking long, slow steps across the front of the classroom.

Her heavy black shoes made deafening thuds through the silence that had fallen instantly over the room. My face fell and I twitched with nerves.

She had Mr Greeny in her hand, and she banged it fiercely into the wooden floor every time she took a step.

I just knew I was going to catch one, and I could tell it was going to be a very bad one. My nerves felt like elastic bands being catapulted around my body as I sat there waiting to hear what sin I had committed, and what penance I would have to pay. Hell was waiting for me, I just knew it. But I wasn't going to die first, I was going to get the roasting of my life right here and now.

Chalkdust puffed up from the floor, making little clouds against Mother Dorothy's black habit as she stomped towards the back of the classroom.

Other kids looked sideways with puzzled expressions on their faces, but they weren't frightened like me. I knew I was the one who was in trouble. I stared into the dark, black stain at the bottom of my inkwell and started to feel nauseous.

Mother Dorothy marched up the steps to the rows of desks at the back, getting closer and closer to mine.

'Does anybody know what that awful smell is?' she demanded. My stomach was doing somersaults by now and I was feeling very hot. I thought I might faint.

'Shall I tell you what it is?' she boomed. She was sniffing very dramatically, as if she had found the source of the foul smell, and she was walking straight towards me with her eyes on fire.

'That smell is dirty knickers!' she shrieked. I was so shocked by what she said I blushed bright scarlet. I could feel my heart pumping blood furiously to my face. Nobody ever talked about underwear in our house, let alone dirty knickers. To hear a nun say that took my breath away.

'You might well feel embarrassed, Cynthia Murphy,' she went on.

'You are the culprit! You are the dirty girl wearing dirty knickers. I can smell them. I can smell your dirty knickers!'

I wanted to shrivel up and die with shame. My palms were sweating, and I hung my head so low the back of my neck ached, but she hadn't finished yet.

'I'm warning you, Cynthia Murphy, wash them out every night, or I'm doing a knicker inspection!' she barked. 'I'm pulling your knickers down and caning you if they are dirty!'

I was wearing the second-hand navy-blue knickers donated to the family by the St Vincent de Paul charity. I knew all too well by now that they marked me out as being from a 'poor' family, and just the thought of the class seeing them made me cringe.

Mother Dorothy hovered over me as if she was waiting for a response, but I was dumbstruck. Even Eileen, who usually shot me a little look of encouragement when I was in the firing line, looked away in utter embarrassment. What could I say? The terrible thing was that I knew my knickers did smell. I only had one pair, and wore them for weeks on end, as Mammy hardly ever did the washing.

I thought Mother Dorothy must know all this, or she wouldn't be telling me to rinse them out myself. Why was she making such a show of me if she knew it wasn't my fault?

Daddy shouted at Mammy and hit her sometimes when his shirts were too filthy for work, and then she would wash them at night when we were all in bed. I don't think she did a good job, because she always did it when she had been drinking for hours and was very tired. I was used to wearing the same dirty clothes all the time.

I tried hard with my work and wanted to read and write well, and not be like Mammy, who had to ask me to write all her lists when she sent me to the shop. It just wasn't fair. Why was I treated so badly?

One day I was struggling with a word in class and asked Mother Felicity to help. She leaned over my copy book and started talking, and as she did so blobs of spit flew out her mouth and landed on my work, making my ink blot all over the page.

I didn't want to be rude and say anything, but when she saw the blots she went mad and slapped me across the face really hard. 'Don't spit on your work, child,' she warned. I was cross and confused. I couldn't believe what had just happened. She had it in for me too. Why? It didn't make any sense.

I dreaded Mother Felicity looking at my work, because she did the same thing every single time. It seemed so weird, and in the end I decided she must enjoy slapping my face and seeing me flinch and cry. There was no other explanation. She had to be mad.

At break time she had another game. She would rummage in the dustbin, find a half-eaten sandwich that was mouldy, and thrust it in my face.

'Be glad you have something to eat,' she warned. 'The black babies in Africa would be glad of that sandwich.'

The way the nuns treated me had made me start to rebel, so once I replied that I would hate to do the black babies out of a bite and handed the sandwich back to her, saying, 'If the babies are so hungry, I wouldn't want to deny them food, so why don't you post it to them?'

She slapped me again for my cheek, but I was glad I stood up for myself, and it gave my friends a bit of a laugh.

I got beaten and called names and was picked on whether I was good or bad, so I thought I might as well have some fun if I was going to be punished anyway.

I worried about my penance though. It still worried me how you knew you'd done enough. I had no idea, and sometimes I said extra Hail Marys or recited the Our Father in my head, hoping it would save me from hell and purgatory and eternal damnation. I didn't want to end up there, I really didn't. Those things sounded worse than any of Mammy and Daddy's fights or beatings, or any punishment the nuns could give me.

In one lesson, Mother Dorothy announced to the class that we were all preparing for our First Holy Communion. I knew this was a really special event and that all little girls making their Communion wore beautiful white dresses. I couldn't quite believe I was going to be one of those little girls. Maybe it would make me holier too, and less likely to burn in hell?

My head filled up with images of myself parading through the village to honour the Blessed Virgin Mary. In my daydream I was wearing a long satin dress and holding a wicker basket full of pretty pink rose petals. I smiled as I took them out of the basket one by one and kissed them before throwing them on the ground behind me.

That's what happened every year at the May procession that took place before the Holy Communion. I'd seen it several times, never dreaming I'd be taking part myself one day. People hung out yellow and white papal flags from their windows and on the street lamps and smiled and waved as the children paraded past their houses.

I started to worry about where my dress would come from and how I would explain why my mammy wasn't in church when I took the holy bread for the first time, because I knew Mammy wouldn't come, even to such a big event in my life. I wasn't sure how I would get round those problems, but I was determined I would have my special day somehow.

To help us prepare for the big event, Mother Dorothy staged a mock confession in the class. She pretended to be the priest and asked us to confess our sins, telling us, 'If you do not tell the truth, God will know and strike you dead!'

My heart skipped a beat. I didn't know what to confess, but I knew I had to come up with something fast, as Mother Dorothy was waiting. I desperately tried to think. I didn't want to be struck dead, and I started to quiver with nerves as my mind raced.

What had I done wrong? I didn't want to mention my dirty clothes or my hair, but that was all I could think of because that's what Mother Dorothy went on about all the time. Then I remembered. I'd pinched a pencil from the school office because Mammy wouldn't buy me one and Mother Dorothy had given me steam for not having the right equipment.

Thank goodness I had a confession to make! I blurted out my sin, thinking it was saving me from being struck down dead, but Mother Dorothy's face twisted with anger. I realized my mistake straight away and my blood ran cold. In that instant the thought of another of Mother Dorothy's punishments seemed a fate worse than death, but that's what I had to accept.

'I won't let her spoil my big day,' I thought as she slapped my face, called me a wicked thief and an evil sinner and sent me outside, telling me I wasn't fit to sit with the other children. 'I don't care,' I thought. 'She can't hurt me! Nothing is going to spoil my Holy Communion.'

I was going to be special for the day. Although Mother Dorothy had me frightened, maybe God might listen to my prayers more now I was big enough to eat the holy bread? Maybe Mammy and Daddy would stop fighting and hitting me?

Chapter 4

A New Dress

'Mammy, Daddy, can you believe I'm taking my First Holy Communion!' I blurted out. I'd been thinking about it non-stop, and couldn't help myself, even though I knew they would show no interest and might even punish me for mentioning it. They must know about it, because it was such a big event in every Catholic child's life, but they had said nothing.

Normally, I kept out of Mammy and Daddy's way, sensing they didn't want me near them, but it was Friday night, and Daddy had come home to give Mammy some housekeeping money before he went to the pub. This was about as good as it ever got in 4 White's Villas. Mammy was standing at the sink stirring a pot of thin stew, humming along to Jim Reeves on the radio. Getting money always made her happy.

'Well, aren't you the big grown-up girl?' she replied. She sounded weird. I never trusted her moods. Sometimes she

Cynthia Owen

said one thing and then did another, or lost her temper without warning. Maybe she was being sarcastic, I wasn't sure.

'Here, take five shillings and your pocket money,' she said, holding out a clenched fist to me and dropping the coins in my stretched-out palm. 'Go and buy a bag of sweets to share, and fetch a bottle of lemonade while you're at it.'

Daddy didn't argue, so I grabbed the money quickly before either of them changed their mind. All us kids were meant to get a few shillings pocket money every week, but sometimes we had to trail round the pubs asking Daddy for it if he forgot to leave it for us, or if he didn't come home after work. Having sweets and lemonade was a rare treat, and for Mammy and Daddy to be standing in the same room without arguing felt like an even bigger treat.

It was obvious I needed a dress for my Holy Communion dress. Was now a good time to talk about it? I'd never had a new dress in my life before, but my teacher Mother Clara had told us all to bring in our dresses for a rehearsal next week, so I had to have one, didn't I? I wasn't sure if I'd be forced to wear the one from Mammy's side of the family, or if that would be too old and dirty. Should I ask them now, while they were calm? I wasn't sure. The atmosphere in the house suddenly felt so alien it made me feel uneasy.

I didn't want to push my luck, so I decided to get the sweets and the lemonade first, and risk mentioning my new dress later, just in case it made them mad and they took the money back off me. Then I'd be in trouble with my brothers and sisters, and if we started fighting Mammy and Daddy would get even madder. I didn't want anybody to get hit, and I really didn't want a beating myself, not when I was going to be dressing up and parading in front of the town.

When I got home with the goodies, breathless from running all the way to the corner shop, Daddy had gone to the pub. Mammy ordered me upstairs. I ran up quickly, hoping I wasn't in trouble and not wanting to miss out on my share of the sweets and lemonade.

I pushed open the bedroom door and saw a tatty carrier bag on the end of my bed. I peeped inside nervously, and found a brand-new pair of shiny black shoes and some knee-length socks, as dazzling white as any the girls at school wore. Dumped in a pile next to them were a pretty little handbag, a pair of gloves and a long veil. Everything shimmered and looked snow-white against the dirty grey sheet on my bed. I stood there for what felt like ages, just staring at them and not daring to touch them, in case somehow they weren't real and were going to disappear.

I had never had a new pair of shoes before. I'd never even had a new pair of socks. And as for the handbag, gloves and veil – well, I couldn't believe my luck.

I pulled on the socks and giggled with glee when I felt the soft cotton kiss my toes. My feet were black with grime, but they felt clean and neat in the new socks. The shoes fitted perfectly too. I thought they looked as shiny as the black pebbles on the beach, after the sea had just washed over them.

'Here's your dress, Cynthia,' Mammy announced. I hadn't heard her come into the room, and her voice made me jump, because it suddenly sounded hard. I felt my spine stiffen as I turned round.

Mammy thrust a crumpled, faded, yellow bundle at me and in a stern voice that was not to be argued with said: 'It has been handed down through all the girls in the family.'

The dress looked like an old rag, and I felt tears fizzing up behind my eyeballs. I wanted to blurt out: 'How many girls? How many years?' but I held my quivering tongue. Mammy would kill me and call me an ungrateful little bitch. I wanted to go downstairs and eat sweets with my brothers and sisters. I didn't want to be hit or called names.

'Thank you, Mammy,' I said quietly, blinking rapidly to push the tears back inside my head. When she left the room I took off the socks and shoes and sobbed silently into my veil.

The following week, Mother Clara told us all to bring in our dresses for a rehearsal. I dawdled all the way to school, the faded dress shoved into a tatty old laundry bag. It felt like I was carrying around a shameful secret. As I arrived I caught glimpses of net underskirts fluttering in the breeze, escaping from the bottom of fancy suit-carriers being proudly paraded into school by the other girls.

I was dreading the moment Mother Clara would tell us to put our dresses on, but I made up my mind I wasn't going to let it break me. 'It doesn't matter,' I told myself firmly. 'Nothing is going to spoil my First Holy Communion. I have a veil and a handbag, and new gloves and socks and shoes! I'll puff out the veil and make it hide the dress. Yes! That's what I'll do.'

I realized I had toughened up a lot since I started school. I had been humiliated and bullied so many times by Mother Dorothy that I couldn't possibly let it get to me every day, or I would have just ended up as crumpled and ragged as my dress, and then she would have won.

I didn't want her to win, so I put on a brave face. When the time came to put on my dress, I pushed back my shoulders and tried to hold my head high. I could hear other girls oohing and aahing over each others' dresses while I shuffled along at the back, desperately trying to make myself look proud and decent when all I really wanted to do was disappear.

The rehearsal was an awful ordeal. 'Focus on what you are actually doing, girls!' Mother Clara instructed. 'You are taking the body of Christ for the very first time. It is a momentous occasion in your life! You are receiving Christ!'

I thought about nothing but my terrible dress, and when we practised eating the holy bread it stuck to the roof of my mouth like cardboard because I was so parched with nerves and tension. When the posh girls gave me sideways glances, nudging each other and sniggering behind their hands, I looked them straight in the eye and bit the inside of my cheek so I didn't cry. 'Don't you dare cry,' I warned myself. 'Then they would win. Don't cry. Be brave.'

Afterwards, Mother Clara took me to one side and whispered that she would like to make me a new dress. I guessed she must have felt sorry for me, but I was too relieved and delighted to feel embarrassed by her pity.

'Yes please!' I said gratefully. 'Thank you so much, Mother Clara. That is so very kind of you!'

It was kind of her, but it gave me another problem.

I walked home full of trepidation as to what Mammy would say. I knew she would go mad. I decided the best way to break the news was to make it sound as unimportant as possible. I just had to come out with it.

'Oh yeah – did I tell you, Mammy?' I said casually. 'Mother Clara is going to make me a new Holy Communion dress... that's kind, isn't it?'

Mammy immediately sat up. Her eyes were blank and her lips set in a mean snarl.

'We do not accept charity, Cynthia. You cannot accept it. Do you hear me? Tell that nun to keep her nose out of our family business.'

I gasped, and then my lungs shrank in my chest so quickly I felt as if I'd been punched. 'Yes, Mammy,' I muttered, not meaning it. There was no way in the world I was going to wear that tatty dress when I was having one made especially for me. Mammy was wrong, and I was going to have to get her to change her mind. It wasn't true that we didn't accept charity. Most things I wore were left on the doorstep in bags. I wasn't going to give in! It was even worth a beating, as long as I got to wear my new dress.

The following week, Mother Clara asked me to stay behind after class one day. 'I'm sure you'll love the dress,' she said kindly, opening a cupboard. It was neatly wrapped in fine tissue paper, and when I peeled the paper back I jumped in the air and threw my hands over my mouth to stop myself squealing.

It was the most beautiful dress I had ever seen. It had a huge puffed-out skirt and flowing, long sleeves, just like something out of a fairytale book. I knew exactly what I was going to do.

Wrapping it up again, I cradled the dress carefully in my arms and took it straight home to show Mammy. 'When she sees this, surely she won't be able to refuse?' I prayed, knowing deep down she was never going to change her mind.

It probably wasn't a great moment to talk to Mammy, but I had no time to spare. She looked very tired, lying in her bed. She was wearing smudged red lipstick, and I'd heard her argue for ages with Daddy last night. I thought back to how I had practised my Hail Mary and Our Father while they fought until late, asking God to make them stop, but it didn't work.

I remembered Mammy called Daddy a 'fuckin' bastard', and he called her a 'fuckin' stupid cow'. She screeched so loudly I could hear her voice vibrate through my huddled-up body, and she kept saying the same things over and over again, getting louder and louder.

When Daddy finally came to bed, I heard him use the toilet bucket and throw his clothes on the floor in a temper. I didn't

---

Cynthia Owen

like it when he sounded so angry. He never spoke to me when I was in bed, and it wasn't that I was afraid of him beating me, because he never beat me in bed.

I just didn't feel comfortable when he was in a bad mood, huffing and puffing and cursing Mammy under his breath. It made me itch my skin nervously, and I lay awake for hours.

Now it was the next day, though, and my thoughts snapped back to the silken dress I had carried home from school like a precious baby clasped to my chest. I had to show Mammy. I had to get her to change her mind.

I asked Mammy if she would like a cup of tea, thinking that might cheer her up after the row with Daddy last night. I put in two extra big sugars and carried the mug upstairs carefully. I gave her a smile when she pushed herself up in bed, took a deep breath and told her I had some great news.

'Look, Mammy! Look at the dress Mother Clara made for me! I know you said we don't accept charity but… isn't it just the most gorgeous dress you've ever seen?'

'It's no different to the one I gave you,' was her dead-eyed reaction. 'You're not to wear that new dress, Cynthia. I forbid it. You can take it back and tell that nun you already have a perfectly good dress, worn by all the Murphy girls.'

'But, but…yes, Mammy,' I said politely, but my mind was already ticking over, hatching another plot.

I rehearsed my plan a hundred times in my head, and when my Communion day came I dutifully put on the old yellow dress.

68

Daddy and Esther were already waiting in the hallway for me when I ran upstairs at the very last moment to show Mammy how I looked.

She was staying in bed, even though it was a very special occasion celebrated across the whole town, but I didn't care. It gave me just the excuse I needed to put my plan into action.

There was an old nail jutting out of the wooden headboard on her bed, and when I ran in to show her the dress I 'accidentally' tore it on the nail.

'Oh, Mammy! What am I to do? There's no time to sew it up. Daddy and Esther are waiting and...oh I suppose I'll just have to wear that other dress after all...'

Mammy started calling me a clumsy cow, but it was early in the day and she didn't shift from her bed to stop me changing, just as I expected. Moments later I was dashing out of the house in the new dress. I waved to the neighbours and called out to every friend I spotted all along the route to the Church of the Assumption in Dalkey. This was my big day, and I wanted everyone to see me in all my finery.

The church was packed out, and whispers whipped off the stone floor and up and down the wooden pews. The priest chimed the little bell to signal it was time for us take our First Holy Communion, and my tummy knotted with nerves.

When I finally took the bread it melted in my mouth. Time stood still as I shimmered in my dress and smiled bravely at the congregation, just like all my classmates. I jutted out my chin proudly. I had been right. Nothing had spoilt my day, not even the fact I was the only child without her mammy watching. I pushed that thought straight out of my head. It didn't matter. Daddy and Esther were here.

After church, I played in the street outside our house for a bit. I knew all the other children who had made their First Communion with me were having big family parties, but we never had parties, even for birthdays. Once, my Uncle Frank, a baker who was married to my mum's older sister, Mag, brought round a cake for my birthday, but Mammy never did anything for me. She usually sent me to the Golden Gift Shop in the village to buy a present if it was one of my brothers' birthdays, but when it was my turn I was only allowed to buy a card. Then Mammy would make me write in it myself: 'Happy Birthday to Cynthia'.

I had already told myself not to expect a present or a card for my Communion. Then I couldn't be disappointed. I figured the best chance I had of enjoying my day was to stay out of the house for as long as possible. That way Mammy couldn't say anything nasty or hit me. She couldn't make me take the dress off. And she couldn't make me do any chores.

So I hung around outside and joined in a game of 'two balls' with my friend from round the corner. It was one of my favourite games, throwing the balls up against the wall one after the other and chanting, 'Ten girl's names that I should know, wish me luck and away I go'. I had to say ten girl's names without stopping and go on to nine boy's names, eight colours, seven flowers and so on, and when I made a mistake it was someone else's turn. None of my friends asked me why I was out in the street on my Holy Communion day playing 'two balls' in my long dress, instead of having a family party. I loved them for that.

Later, I was allowed to watch telly while Daddy went to the pub. It was a very old set and was often broken, but today really was my lucky day because it was working and I was allowed to choose what I wanted to watch. Mammy always liked to watch the news. She hardly ever went out of the house, and I think it was her way of keeping up with what went on in the neighbourhood. She couldn't read the news-papers, but she loved to gossip about local goings-on, and so she watched the local news whenever she could.

But today she was still upstairs, and I was still in the dress and was choosing what to watch on telly. I sat neatly on the sofa, crossed my ankles and clutched my handbag and gloves on my lap, feeling like a proper little lady.

Little House on the Prairie, *Heidi* and *Pippi Longstocking* were my favourite shows, and I was delighted to find that an episode of *Heidi* was just starting. It was as if she'd been waiting for me to come in!

Heidi was running across a beautiful open mountainside with rosy cheeks, wearing a fresh cotton dress and shiny shoes, laughing and smiling without a care in the world.

In that moment, I imagined I was Heidi. I had the dress and the shiny shoes, didn't I? I jumped up and looked in the mirror above the fireplace. I wanted to check if I really looked like Heidi, and I grinned as I climbed up onto the arm of a chair to see my reflection.

All day I thought I'd looked my best, but I watched my grin slip as I realized the girl in the dusty mirror didn't have neat plaits and sparkling pearls for teeth like Heidi. Her hair was tatty and dirty, and her teeth were covered in black and yellow smudges.

'Cynthia, will you get up here and take that bloody dress off?' Mammy yelled. 'Didn't I tell you not to watch TV when I'm upstairs? Get up here now if you don't want a beating! Where's your father? Has he gone off to the pub, the drunken bastard…'

I was back to being Cynthia Murphy, and suddenly the sour, stale smell that hung in the air caught in my throat. I wanted to be sick. I would never be like Heidi, and I would never be happy. It wasn't even worth dreaming about.

Chapter 5

Bye-bye, Esther

I cried when I heard the news that Esther was leaving home – she had got a job and was off to start a new life in Wales. I looked at my feet and sniffled. There must have been about seven or eight of us in the house at that moment, but I felt very lonely, as if Esther had already sailed away and I was left all alone with nobody to care for me.

'I'll come home for visits, and you can come and visit me, Cynthia,' Esther told me kindly. She smiled, but I thought she looked sad too. I thought of all the times she took me down to the harbour to watch the boats bobbing on the sparkling sea. She took me there in the summer holidays, and on sunny weekends too.

I loved the summer, but I hated being stuck in our cramped and gloomy house with no sunlight coming in. The hot weather meant we could spend hours outside every day. Esther took me to the park too, pushing me high on the swings. I felt like a little butterfly, flitting through the air, as light as a feather.

The weight I felt pressing on my shoulders at home was always lifted a bit when I was outdoors. I didn't even realize how heavy my shoulders normally felt until I was outside and felt the knots in my neck slip open, one by one. I loved being able to breathe fresh air. I loved going to the beach and splashing in the sea, and I loved the tingly, clean feeling I had when the sun dried my back as I sat on the sand. I never felt so clean as I did on the beach.

Esther taught me how to swim. She held my hand walking home, and she taught me how to look left and right when I crossed the road. She talked to me, asked me questions and listened to my answers. I could ask her things like 'What is your favourite colour?' and she would think about it properly and give me an answer, instead of swearing at me or telling me to 'shut up nagging'. Then she'd say: 'What's your favourite colour, Cynthia? Tell me, why do you like yellow?'

I knew I was really going to miss Esther, and I had a little ache in my chest whenever I thought about her leaving. Instead of us watching the boats together, she would be crossing the sea to another country, leaving me behind. It wasn't long now. I knew I had to get used to it, but I could hardly bear the thought.

For a little while now, Esther and I had been sharing the single bed while Mammy and Daddy had the double bed on the other side of the front bedroom. Mary and Martin sometimes slept in that room too, sharing the big blue cot that once belonged to me and Peter. There were never enough beds to go round in our house. Every bed had pillows at both ends so you could top and tail, and you never knew when the sleeping plans might change.

I loved the time I had sharing that single bed with Esther. I loved it when I heard her climb into bed after me. I felt safe next to her, and I enjoyed feeling her warmth in the bed. The shouting downstairs never felt so loud or so scary when Esther was there.

It wasn't long after my sister left that Daddy started sleeping in the single bed with me. It seemed strange, but I said nothing. I was only eight-years-old.

'You're to sleep in the single bed again tonight, d'you hear me?' Mammy said in a voice that wasn't to be questioned or argued with, but I didn't like it. It was very uncomfortable as there wasn't enough room for us both. Daddy got too close and moved in that funny shuffling way that frightened me.

Mammy hardly ever looked at me when she spoke. Her sunken eyes looked like they had a fine yellow film stuck on them. I never asked her anything much, and I didn't dare question her on this, but something didn't seem right.

I was starting to accept that Mammy wasn't interested in me at all. She'd told me loads of times that she didn't like me, and that I was her 'least favourite' child, and now I started to think it must be true. Not going to my Holy Communion had shown me she didn't care about my feelings at all.

Sometimes, when her relatives from the north of Dublin or England visited, she got herself dressed up in her prettiest dress and went to the pub wearing her red lipstick and swinging a black patent-leather handbag. I'd seen her potter round the garden too, planting geraniums and gossiping with neighbours over the garden wall.

Occasionally, very rarely, she and Daddy disappeared together in the evening. They said they went to where Daddy worked. They said he had 'business' to attend to, but they always came back staggering like they had had lots of drinks, with Mammy draped over Daddy's shoulders and laughing, just how I imagined they must have looked when they were courting.

Whatever they did there, it seemed to make Mammy giddy and happy for a little while. It was the only time she didn't seem to hate Daddy, and he seemed happy too, because he bought Mammy sherry afterwards, and gave her extra house-keeping money. Those moments didn't happen very often at all, but I'd seen enough to know that Mammy could leave the house if she wanted to.

That meant she just couldn't be bothered to come to my Holy Communion, didn't it? She could have put up with people 'looking down their noses at us' in church if she'd wanted to be there on my big day. She'd told me she hated me lots of times, but I always hoped she didn't mean it and that she just called me a 'bitch' and a 'liar' and a 'devil child' when she was tired or cross. But Mammy had stayed in bed on my First

Holy Communion. She must really hate me to miss my special day like that.

After a while, Mammy changed her mind and told me that I was to sleep in the double bed now. I didn't understand. Why was she telling me to sleep in the bed with Daddy? Why did she want me in her place if she hated me so much and thought so little of me?

I was nervous, but I knew not to argue with Mammy about anything. I undressed slowly, feeling sick and scared as I climbed into the big, sagging bed for the first time.

It was cold inside, and I wrapped my arms around myself to get warm. I could smell smoke and sweat and Daddy's Old Spice aftershave, and it wasn't nice at all.

I didn't feel comfortable, what with the cold and the smells and the rough feel of the dirty covers on my body.

It was dark in the room, but I could see spots of blood on the bedlinen and strained my eyes to make out what the unfamiliar stains on the bottom sheet were. I wondered what it was that stuck to the grey cotton and made it feel stiff and nasty. I wasn't comfortable at all, but as I lay there all alone I forced myself to think of something nice, to try to stop myself feeling so worried and afraid. What was I worried about? Surely being allowed to sleep in the big bed meant I wasn't in the bad books for a change? Maybe it was meant to be a treat?

I desperately tried to imagine myself at the beach, my favourite place, to make myself feel less scared. I pictured myself jumping in the waves, with Mammy holding my hand and Daddy smiling on the beach. Nobody was shouting. Nobody was arguing. Nobody was calling me names or hitting me. I could smell fresh air, and I could taste tangy salt in the sea breeze. I was clean and I was happy. The scene was very hard to imagine, and my head hurt as I desperately tried to cling on to the image. It felt so unreal and so unbelievable I just couldn't hold it, and the picture slipped away, leaving my head full of dark clouds, like it usually was. Even dreaming of happiness was impossible, and I slowly dropped off to sleep, feeling as terrified as ever.

Daddy's buckle hitting the hard lino woke me up. The clank of the metal triggered a reaction in my brain even when I was in a deep sleep. It was a sound that always came before a beating, but when I peeped through my half-closed eyes I knew straight away that I wasn't going to get a beating. I remembered I was in the big bed, and I told myself it had to be some kind of privilege, even if I didn't know why I was there. Nobody was going to beat me, Daddy never beat me in bed. Bed was the one place you were safe from a beating.

I sighed sleepily to myself when I heard Daddy get into the bed. I was lying on my side, and I felt the mattress give a little ripple beneath me as he tucked himself in behind me. It had to be past midnight, because Daddy never came home from the pub until that time. I shut my eyes tight and pretended to be fast asleep.

Daddy was breathing very loudly. Even when he tucked

himself up close to me when I had slept in the same bed as him before, I hadn't heard him breathe so loudly. I wasn't used to feeling him quite so close.

In the daytime, he never came near me. I'd never sat on his knee or even held his hand. The only time he touched me was when he grabbed hold of my arm to hold me still while he beat the back of my thighs with his leather belt.

My heart started to beat a bit faster, like it did when I could tell Mammy was cross and was going to hit me. I knew Daddy wasn't going to hit me though, because I was in the big bed and the belt was on the floor now. No, Daddy wasn't going to hit me. He was going to snuggle up behind me.

Daddy was naked except for his shirt. I could feel the rough cotton and the cold buttons on my back. It felt strange to feel him so close. I could feel the bare skin of his legs pressing against the backs of my own little legs. His skin felt hairy and sweaty, and I didn't like it. It made the scabs on my legs twitch and itch, but I was afraid to scratch them in case Daddy knew I was awake. I could smell Daddy's breath now. It smelled like old beer and the stale ash I had to clear from Mammy's ashtray. It wasn't nice. It made me wrinkle my nose, even though I was trying very hard indeed to look like I was fast asleep. I wished he would move back a bit so I didn't have to breathe in his smell.

I couldn't seem to escape it though. Daddy's smell and the sweat on his skin felt as if it was clinging to me, from the back of my heels to the top of my scalp. He had packed himself in so closely behind me I felt trapped. I couldn't complain though, could I? Mammy would call me an 'ungrateful little bitch'. She always called me that if I dared to grumble about anything, like the watery, gristle-filled stew she cooked, or the 'new' clothes she gave me with sleeves down to my fingertips and holes under the arms.

I hoped Daddy would fall asleep soon. I'd heard him fall asleep so many times after I'd waited for him to get in from the pub or I'd listened to him fight with Mammy. I normally found it hard to get to sleep myself until I'd heard his chesty, spluttering breathing slow down and settle into a steady rhythm. That's what usually happened. He coughed his guts up most nights, choking on the last drag of his cigarette while he used the toilet bucket. Then he would fill his lungs with a tight gasp before falling into a wheezy, purring sleep.

That hadn't happened tonight. After his belt hit the floor I heard him cough and spit something into the toilet bucket, emptying his rattling throat. But his breathing got heavier and faster when he got into bed. Now he was sort of puffing and panting, and it felt like he was pushing himself closer and closer into my back, closer than he ever had before. I could feel his hot, smelly breath sticking to the back of my neck, gusting through my hair and making my scalp prickle.

What could I do? Now the pushing had become harder, and Daddy was sort of rubbing himself into my back, worse than he had before when we were in the same bed. What was he doing? It felt like he was touching me with a part of his body I didn't recognize. It felt so strange. I didn't like it. It made me feel wary of Daddy, but I didn't dare speak or move.

Finally, Daddy stopped and pulled away from me. I lay there like a little motionless doll, not wanting to give any sign I was awake in case he drew closer to me again. I didn't even want to breathe in case I caught his attention, so I took shallow, silent little sips of air as I listened to Daddy turn over, shuffle himself away from me and, at last, take the loud, wheezing purrs of sleep I longed to hear.

The next morning, Mammy was in the bed fast asleep, and Daddy was gone. I was relieved to see Mammy there instead of Daddy, although normally I was much more scared of her than him. She was in a deep sleep, with her hair sprawled out like a mass of wild flowers on the pillow. She looked peaceful and pretty, not scary at all.

Sleeping in Mammy and Daddy's bed wasn't how I expected. I wondered how long it would last, and told myself not to worry about what Daddy did. It must just be what daddies do.

At school, Mother Dorothy announced that we were going on a trip to Howth in North Dublin. I'd never been on a school trip and was delighted. Mother Dorothy told us the ancient St Mary's Church was in Howth. It was centuries old and dedicated to the Blessed Virgin Mary. 'So we'll be having no bold behaviour,' she threatened. 'You are very lucky children to be taken on such a trip. Now go home and ask your mammies and daddies to pay their contribution. We shall be going by bus, and you are to bring your own lunch.'

I left school that day feeling nervous but excited. I'd been a good girl and had not complained about anything Daddy did. I'd scrubbed the dishes before school, and I'd bought Mammy some bread and cigarettes at lunchtime. I'd helped clean up the little ones, Mary and Martin, and given them their milk too.

Now it was 4 p.m., and I was wondering how best to mention the money for the trip. I thought it was best to do my other jobs first, then ask Mammy nicely.

'Cynthia, you're to go to the off licence in the next village for me,' Mammy bellowed from the top of the stairs as soon as I walked into the house.

'I need some cider! I've heard it's cheaper than at the off licence in Dalkey! Here, Cynthia, take the money and go and get it for your mammy. Don't go buying any sweets now! I want every scrap of change, or you won't know what's hit you!'

I did as I was told, because arguing with Mammy simply wasn't an option. I knew I had to do as she said, or all hell would break out. I decided I would get the cider as quickly as possible, and when Mammy was happily drinking it I would tell her I needed money for the school trip. I didn't realize it until later, but the off licence was about three miles away – and all to save a few shillings!

The weather started to turn bad almost as soon as I set out. I was wearing my now old and battered Holy Communion shoes, but the leather had worn so thin that rainwater was leaking in, making my toes wrinkle up like little wet raisins. I ran at first, thinking I'd get the job done quicker, but soon the rain felt like it was hammering straight into my skin, making me heavy and soggy and driving me back. My fingers turned ice-blue as I clutched the coins tight, and I had to keep swapping hands so I didn't go completely numb and drop the money down into the streams of water washing down the street.

It started getting very dark on my way back. I couldn't tell the time, but it felt like I'd been out for hours. Every time I turned a corner a bit more light faded, like doors were shutting at the end of streets. My stomach was twisting with hunger and I was shivering with cold. With every sodden step I told myself it would be worth it to please Mammy and get my money to see the sights of Howth. I wasn't sure I was interested in seeing that ancient church. I wasn't sure if worshipping the Blessed Virgin Mary would ever help my prayers be heard and stop the fighting and shouting at home. But there was a castle and a lighthouse and glorious views over Dublin Bay. And we were going by bus!

I'd only ever been to Dublin once before, with Daddy on a Christmas-shopping trip. It was like something out of a storybook, and I'd kept pinching myself and wondering if it was real, because Daddy had never taken me anywhere before. I still don't know why he did it. It was a complete surprise, and he didn't shout at me or tell me off once.

Remembering the Christmas trip cheered me up. I'm sure Daddy smiled when we looked at the lights and displays in the shop windows, and he even took me into Woolworth's for a mug of milk and a pink wafer biscuit. Every detail was etched in my memory, because it was such an unusual thing for Daddy to do. If Mammy let me go on that trip, I was sure she would let me do another one.

At last I was back from the off licence. Falling through the back door with the cider tucked under my dripping cardie, I felt like I'd marched to the top of Howth Castle and defeated a whole army of those Norman invaders Mother Dorothy told us about. I'd never been so glad to get home in my life before.

'Here you go, Mammy,' I said proudly, holding out the bottle like a trophy.

'Where the bloody hell have you been?' she screamed back. 'You've been gone for fuckin' ages! I've been waitin' hours for my cider! Couldn't you have gone any quicker, you lazy little bitch' She grabbed the bottle and thumped me sharply in the ear.

I shrieked with pain and cowered in the kitchen, watching nervously as she twisted off the metal bottle top with her teeth, poured herself a large tumblerful and took a long, slow slug of the cider.

She sat back in her rocking chair, and I was sure I saw her face soften a bit. The deep frown lines between her eyes seemed to fade as the golden liquid slid down her throat.

Steeling myself to take a few steps towards her, with the

sound of blood pumping noisily through my smarting ear, I asked gingerly: 'Mammy, I was wonderin', could I have some money to go to Howth? Mother Dorothy says we're all to pay a contribution, as we're going on a bus and we're going to see a holy church and...'

'No way!' Mammy screeched. 'Where in God's name do you think I'm going to get that kind of money from? Do you think I'm made of money? Do you think it grows on trees? You're such a selfish cow, Cynthia. If I were to pay for you to go gallivanting off to Howth, you'd be taking food out of the babies' mouths. Tell that interfering nun you can't go. No way!'

She swigged greedily from her glass and slammed it down. 'Get yourself to bed. Get out of my sight!'

I stripped off my soaked clothes and lay shivering in bed, hot tears streaming down my cheeks and running into the cold rainwater trickling from my hair.

I thought about telling Mother Dorothy the truth. 'My Mammy hates me! She won't let me go on the trip! She says we can't afford it, but she drinks cider! She smokes lots of cigarettes! It's not fair!'

Instead, the next day I tiptoed into her office like a poor church mouse, scuttling along quietly so as not to be seen by the other children as I tapped on the door. 'I'm sorry, Mother Dorothy. My family cannot afford to send me on the trip,' I muttered. 'I'm afraid I can't go.'

Mother Dorothy sighed deeply, as if I was testing her

patience to the limit. She looked me up and down several times, scowling and tutting and shaking her head from side to side.

I thought she might reach for her cane, and I started to feel jittery.

'Very well, the school will make an exception and fund the trip,' she snapped.

I wasn't sure what she meant at first and stood there quaking, hanging my head in shame.

'I said you can go on the trip, child! You do not have to pay. I will let you go for free. Do you understand? Are you not grateful? Well then?'

I couldn't believe my ears. Mammy just had to provide a packed lunch.

'Bring some bread and butter and a bottle of water like all the other children,' Mother Dorothy bellowed. 'That is all you need, child. Be off with you now! And be thankful! Thank the Lord for your good fortune!'

Mammy liked money, but she didn't like to spend it on us kids. In fact the more money she had, it seemed, the more alcohol she drank, or the fancier the bottles it came in. Whenever I heard her shouting 'Where's the fuckin' money?' to Daddy she complained that she had to 'make do' with whatever alcohol she could afford.

Yet when I told her about the free trip she still wasn't happy with me. I thought she'd be pleased I wouldn't be taking away her drinking and smoking money, or housekeeping for the little ones' milk, and that the nuns wouldn't be knocking on the door and shaming the family, asking why I didn't pay the contribution. In fact, she was furious about the nuns dishing out charity. 'Haven't I told you, we don't take charity!' she screamed. Thankfully, she didn't go so far as banning me from going on the trip, and when she ordered me upstairs to the double bed I was relieved to get out of her way. 'Off you go now. Hurry up and no messin' about,' she shouted. 'Up those stairs now!'

I felt uncomfortable to be in the double bed again and couldn't sleep. I tried to think of good things to stop myself feeling worried about Daddy tucking himself in too close to me again, as I was sure he would when he eventually came in from the pub.

I thought about the school trip and my Christmas shopping with Daddy, and as the minutes and hours dragged by my mind flicked back to another Christmas. It might have been when I was four or five. I remembered waking up on Christmas morning and seeing something glistening in the dark. A stray shard of light had managed to break through the only slither of window not covered by the black blanket, and it was making halos of light as it hit something shiny. When I tiptoed over to get a closer look I clattered my shins into something hard and round and rubbery. It was a trike! It had a little basket on the handlebars and it was brand-new. I couldn't believe such a shiny, new gift was for me. I'd never had such a big present in my life before. I was thrilled. Lying in bed now, I remembered how it wasn't long before some boys took the back wheels off it to make themselves a trolley, and I was heartbroken. But at least it was mine for a while. I tried to hold on to the happy memory, not the bad one, but still I felt nervous lying in that bed.

Daddy's key twisting in the front-door lock snapped all my memories from my mind.

I quivered as I felt my nerves wake up and start to jangle. How should I feel about being sent to the big bed again? I didn't know as it all kept changing. Perhaps I was worrying too much, but I couldn't help myself, especially as it kept on happening. A few nights earlier, Daddy had climbed into bed with me. I think it must have been very late indeed, because I couldn't remember much about it. My head was thick with sleep when I felt him squeeze in behind me. I didn't remember feeling scared, and I didn't remember him doing anything that felt strange. No, Daddy wasn't going to frighten me. He loved me, didn't he? He must do, or he wouldn't want to sleep next to me.

Daddy was in bed with me now. He'd said something quietly to Mammy downstairs, and she didn't shout. I could hear the chink as Mammy's cider bottle hit the rim of a glass, and the slow chug of the drink filling up her tumbler again.

Daddy was tucking himself in behind me now. Not long, I thought, until I can let myself fall asleep next to Daddy. Just let him get comfortable. Don't wriggle. Don't let him know you are awake in case he gets cross. His breath smelled worse tonight, like he'd eaten something that had gone off. It reminded me of the smell of the plughole in the kitchen sink, when old food and dirty plates had been left all night, or when he had done a wee in there. I tried to take in shallow drops of air through my nose, but his smell was getting nearer. He was pushing himself up against me again, but harder than he did last time. It felt stranger, too, like he was rubbing up and down my whole back. I felt the rubbing on my bottom.

The only noise I could hear was his raspy breathing, which seemed to be getting louder and quicker. It didn't matter. 'Don't let it scare you,' I told myself.

My thoughts stopped dead, as if my brain had suddenly come up against an invisible wall. I felt something warm hit the back of my neck and my hair, but it wasn't Daddy's smelly, burning breath this time. I didn't know what it was, but it made Daddy stop too. He pushed me away from him roughly, and minutes later I heard deep, slow, snores rumbling round the bed.

I touched my head slowly and carefully and didn't like how it felt. There was something sticky and unfamiliar about it. I wiped my hand on the sheet and opened my eyes warily. The inky blackness frightened me and made me snap my eyes shut again, but then I had shapes dancing inside my eyelids. I couldn't escape from the scary blackness, and I lay awake for hours listening to Daddy snore. At least he was asleep. I always felt better when he was asleep.

*   *   *

I was getting told to sleep in Daddy's bed about once or twice every week now. I didn't really like what he did, and my hair was itchier than ever since I slept next to Daddy. It wasn't just the lice. Lying with it damp and sticky after Daddy's close cuddles seemed to give me a rash.

I tried not to think of that when the day of the school trip arrived. This was a real treat, and as I walked behind Mother Dorothy and my classmates, I marvelled at the sights and sounds. Howth was all I dreamed it would be.

We settled in a park for lunch, and I pulled out my bread and butter and bottle of water. It was the first time in my life I'd been allowed to take a packed lunch, and I sat on the grass with my classmates feeling as pleased as Punch.

I was just about to bite into my bread when I felt curious eyes looking my way. It reminded me of the first day I started school. What were they looking at? I immediately thought about my hair. I knew it was messier than normal. It was sort of matted up the back where the itchy rash had bubbled up. Did it look terrible? I glanced around to see why the other girls were staring at me, and my eyes fell on their packed lunches. Instead of carrying their food in a plastic carrier bag, they had colourful tins and tubs. Inside, they had neatly cut sandwiches wrapped in tin foil, bottles of lemonade, home-made oatcakes, crispy apples and squares of chocolate.

I looked down at the grass and saw Mother Dorothy's heavy black clogs stomping towards me out of the corner of my eye. 'Eat up now, children!' she ordered. 'When you've finished your lunch, those of you whose mammies and daddies have allowed you to bring spending money can form a queue at the icecream van.'

My tummy felt scraped out it was so empty. I always had Shredded Wheat or Weetabix for breakfast, with sugar sprinkled on top if there was any left in the packet, but breakfast had been hours ago.

I was starving hungry, but my throat felt like someone had pulled it out, tied a big knot in it and shoved it back down my gullet. It felt so bad I couldn't even chew, let alone swallow. Why had Mother Dorothy told me to bring bread and water when everybody else had treats and goodies? I felt so embarrassed I just wanted to go home.

Watching the other girls run off giggling to the icecream van made me feel so left out I wanted to cry. It wasn't fair. Why did things always get worse when I hoped they'd get better? It simply wasn't worth even hoping things would turn out all right, because they never did.

Chapter 6

'Please Stop, Daddy'

'Cynthia, you're to take your brother Martin to school with you tomorrow. I've enough to cope with without lookin' after him as well!

Tell those nuns I'm sick. I'm too sick to look after him. If he's not with you there's nobody can look after him!'

Martin was just two years old. I looked at him strapped in his stripy nylon pram and felt full of pity. His face was caked in dirt, and he had food stains around his mouth. He was wearing a lilac-coloured sweater that would suit a girl much better, and he had on a pair of faded brown trousers I'd seen go in and out of the cupboard under the stairs lots of times.

'But, Mammy, what will I do with him? What about my lessons? The nuns'll wallop me if I don't pay attention!'

I didn't normally dare answer Mammy back, but this seemed like a terrible idea, especially because I'd been in big trouble at school lately.

Since taking our First Holy Communion, Mother Dorothy had been taking the whole class to attend regular confession.

We'd been taken yesterday, and Mother Dorothy warned us all the way there that we had to confess every one of our sins. 'I don't want to hear any nonsense about you not having committed a sin. You are all sinners. The only way to avoid burning in hell and eternal damnation is to confess your sins.'

I felt panicky when I was led to the confession box, where Father O'Brien sat hunched up in the half-light inside. I didn't know what to say, but I knew I had to come up with something convincing. It wasn't like the mock confession in the classroom, where Mother Dorothy punished me for my confession. This was private, so I didn't have to worry so much about the consequences. But I still had to come up with something.

I quickly invented three imaginary sins in my head and whispered them as quietly as possible. 'I'm sorry, Father, for I have sinned. I stole 10p from my mother's purse.

'I'm sorry, Father, for I have sinned. I stole a copy book from the school office.'

Father O'Brien shook his head solemnly after my first two confessions, repeating them after me in a disgusted voice.

'I'm sorry, Father, for I have sinned. I cursed my mother,' I ended.

'What did you say to curse your mother?' he quizzed me angrily. I felt very uncomfortable, because he spoke very loudly and his voiced echoed around the confession box.

'Well then? What was this curse you used against your mother?'

I wanted to get out of there as quickly as possible. I had to say the first curse that came into my head. It was the one I'd heard Mammy and Daddy say most often: 'Fuck off,' I muttered apologetically.

'You sinful child!' he shouted at the top of his voice. 'You must pray to the Virgin Mary to save your soul. Pray for twenty extra minutes at bedtime and say ten Hail Mary's and two Our Father's!'

I left the confession box with my head bowed in disgrace, and a pair black shoes and the hem of a nun's habit loomed into my line of vision.

I looked up in horror. Mother Dorothy had been standing outside and had clearly heard every single world. Her skin had turned the colour of a ripe plum, and she was so angry she was visibly shaking.

'How dare you! You wicked child!' she blustered, strands of spit wobbling precariously between her lips, like a spider's web caught in the wind.

She grabbed my ear and dragged me to the front of the church, shouting all the way down the aisle: 'You are not fit to sit with the rest of the children! You are a sinner! You are forbidden from talking to the other girls!'

Back in the classroom, she was still apoplectic with rage.

'Cynthia Murphy, come and do this sum on the board!' she goaded. I was still smarting from the humiliation of being told I wasn't worthy of sitting with the other girls, and I hadn't been concentrating at all.

I got the sum wrong, prompting Mother Dorothy to bellow triumphantly: 'I give up! You are a stupid child!' Then, I was sent to stand in a corner wearing a large hat with the letter 'D' on it for dunce.

'When you grow up you'll be standing on the corner under the streetlight!' she snorted loudly. 'You'll go up a lane and come down pushing a pram!'

The other girls looked at each other with puzzled expressions. None of us knew what she meant at all.

Now, as Mammy presented me with Martin in his new pushchair, Mother Dorothy's remark popped into my head, diverting my thoughts from the dilemma of taking my baby brother to school with me.

'Where did you get that pushchair from? Did you get it up a lane?' I asked Mammy curiously.

'What are you goin' on about, Cynthia? Stop talking fuckin' nonsense. You're to take Martin to school in the pushchair. He'll be no trouble strapped in there.'

'I bet you went up a lane, and came down pushing that pram,' I said to Mammy innocently.

Her fist landed on my cheek before I could blink. 'What did you say? Are you callin' me a prostitute?' she crowed.

'I'm sorry, Mammy, Mother Dorothy taught me that saying! I'm sorry, Mammy, of course I'll take Martin to school in the pushchair.'

'I know you will, because I'm saying you will. Calling me a prostitute and blaming your dirty mouth on those holy nuns! You little lying bitch, Cynthia!'

She thumped me again, on the other side of my face, and Martin started to cry and struggle against the straps.

'Oh for fuck's sake, look what you've done now! You've made poor Martin cry!'

That night, when Daddy got into bed beside me, I wondered if he would notice my sore eye and feel sorry for me. It had swollen up where Mammy had hit me, and she had sent me to the chemist to buy a patch.

'Cover your eye with one hand when you are in the shop,' she ordered. I could tell she was worried about me for once, because normally she never let me have a patch or plaster for anything. 'Then cover your bruise with the patch before you walk back down the street. At school tomorrow, tell the nuns you have a stye. I don't want them poking their noses into our business.'

If Daddy did notice my sore eye, it didn't make him any more gentle with me. He rubbed up against me harder than ever that night. I don't think he could have felt sorry for me at all, because this felt like a punishment, and I felt very scared and tearful. He was terrifying me.

I thought about it as I pushed the pram into school the next day. It made my head ache. I just couldn't work it out. I didn't want to think about it, but I couldn't seem to get it out of my mind. My head was itching too, worse than ever.

Martin was crying in the pram. His cries ricocheted round my head and I stared at the cloudy sky in front of me, wishing I could block everything out.

I could hear the girls giggling when I pushed the pram into the classroom: 'What's smelly Cynthia up to this time? Will you look at the state of that baby! What's she thinking of? Has she no shame?'

The voices tried to get inside my brain, but my head felt like it was full of thick, damp sand. I felt very tired and I couldn't think clearly at all.

Did I have no shame? I wasn't sure. I just felt numb and exhausted.

'What have we here, child?' demanded Mother Dorothy, haughtily.

'It's my brother Martin, Mother Dorothy. My mammy says to tell you she's very sick and can't look after him. There's no one else in the house, so I've brought him into class. I'll make sure he's no trouble at all.'

With that, Martin started roaring loudly, tugging at the side of his buggy and shouting, 'Out, out!'

I didn't know what to do. I was eight years old. I tried to rock the buggy discreetly with my foot, while Mother Dorothy stood over the pair of us, glaring.

'Is there no end to your boldness? Settle the child immediately, and if you disrupt the class again there will be severe consequences!'

I wouldn't have minded being sent out of the class that day.

I couldn't focus on a word the teachers said. My foot ached as I rocked the buggy, shushing Martin and pleading with him with my eyes to quieten down. Every time he grumbled and fidgeted, my heart lurched up into my throat.

I hated Mammy for making me bring him. I didn't want to tell lies to the nuns. I didn't want to be made fun of by the other girls. I didn't like the way my head ached with tiredness and itched after Daddy had kept me awake at night. I just wanted to be normal. I looked around and longed to have clean white socks and clean hair, every day, like the other girls.

I wondered why I was the one who always seemed to get lumbered with so many jobs, and caring for the little ones. With Esther gone, things had got worse at home. I was ordered by Mammy to wash the dishes and feed the children. It wasn't fair, but I didn't want Martin or Mary to be hungry or dirty. I loved them, so I cared for them as best I could.

Yet it didn't matter how much I helped or what I said or did, things were always horrible at home, and the rows continued with scary regularity.

I often heard thumps and thuds and slaps and smacks when I was lying in bed at night. Mammy cursed and cried, and Daddy spat and swore while I covered my head under a blanket, praying hard for them to stop.

Wherever I slept, I felt afraid. And it was even worse when Mammy and Daddy had a big row.

That night, I started to tremble when Daddy climbed into bed with me.

I knew he was in a filthy mood, because I'd heard him swearing and cursing at Mammy really badly, so what would happen when he came upstairs tonight?

When I heard the bedroom door open I started gasping for air, as if someone was choking me. I clasped my hands round my body and felt my fingers shaking against my skin.

I was petrified. Something horrible was going to happen. I just knew it. Stay calm, I told myself, over and over again, as I heard him carry out his familiar routine.

The toilet bucket splashed and stank, the belt and zip of his trousers chinked open and his clothes tumbled to the floor. He coughed and spat, and he took a step closer to the bed. I could hear his breathing getting nearer.

Every second brought new fear. My blood was boiling in my head, pulsating around my sore eye.

Daddy was in the bed now, and I braced my spine, expecting him to pull in behind me.

To my horror, he pulled me towards him angrily, turning me to face him as he did so. His jagged fingernails dug into the tops of my arms and I gasped in pain.

It was very black in the room, and I stared into the darkness in silence, waiting to see what would happen next.

I felt sick as Daddy started rubbing me with his body again, like he had done before.

He seemed to be brimming with rage. He was moving his bare body very quickly up and down in front of me. Instead of slamming my eyes shut like I normally did, I stared out desperately into the blackness, looking for clues.

His face was right in front of mine, but he seemed to look straight through me. I couldn't work out what part of his body was in front of me now.

Daddy's breathing was somewhere above my head, and some strange part of him was touching my cheek. It smelled horrible, and I snapped my face away in horror. I didn't want him that close to me, but he was pushing right into my face.

I wanted to shout out and beg him to stop, but I was petrified of making a noise and angering him more. I was afraid of opening my mouth, but it was no use. Daddy was forcing it open, and somehow he was pushing part of himself inside.

I turned my head desperately, trying to avoid him, but Daddy was very strong and I couldn't get away. I felt something spill on the sides of my mouth. It freaked me out completely. My stomach somersaulted and I retched.

This felt all wrong, but Daddy seemed to be very calm now. He had already pushed himself away and was breathing deeply, like he was in a nice sleep. I was shaking with fright, but I also felt very relieved that Daddy had settled down and left me alone.

Was he supposed to do that to me? I really wasn't sure, and I lay there for a very long time thinking about it, wishing I didn't have that horrible taste in my mouth.

And so it continued. Again and again I was forced to sleep next to Daddy. As night after night ended in the same routine,

I wondered why he was doing it, and whether Mammy knew anything about it.

Now I knew all too well that a sleep in the big bed meant more bad things, so whenever Mammy said: 'Cynthia – you're to sleep in the double bed tonight,' my stomach knotted up tightly. I knew I was in for a night of terror, a night of Daddy doing things I didn't like and didn't understand.

I would lie there afraid, trying to pretend to be asleep. My mind started to race. I really hoped Daddy wouldn't touch my mouth again. It made me feel so sick and scared, and I felt dirty and horrible afterwards.

I hoped he wouldn't do anything to me. It was all terrifying. My mind would flick around, remembering everything he had done, all at once, and all my memories would tumble into one big pot of wet sludge that milled about inside my skull.

Mammy had started giving me some of her cider. I wondered why, because she loved her cider so much. 'Here you go, Cynthia, take a big long drink of this before you get in the double bed tonight.' I didn't like the strong appley taste, but I didn't want to upset Mammy and waste any. 'Drink it all up!' she ordered, so I did.

It felt as though the liquid was slopping about inside my skull, and my brain was swimming, lots of scary memories colliding inside.

He had started to do so many new things that hurt and frightened me. Every night, I went to bed and prayed for sleep to come and rescue me from the horror that was in store. But it never did.

Instead, I listened out for his footsteps on the stairs, the sound that signalled the beginning of another night of fear and confusion. It was the darkness that really did it. In the pitch black of the room, the things he did to me burned into my brain.

I am not sure exactly how long it was after he'd done that thing to my mouth, but Daddy had started to make me touch his body. I remembered him pushing my hand down in between his legs. It felt so disgusting I started to cry.

He tried to wrap my fingers around him, but they were too small and I struggled. The more I struggled the harder he pushed my hand down. My fingers felt so tiny. I was sure I shouldn't be touching him there. Mammy told me 'private parts' were filthy and dirty. Daddy was trying to make me rub him, the way he rubbed himself up and down my back and around my mouth. Please stop, Daddy. I wanted to say it, but how would he react? I wasn't brave enough to speak.

Mammy had given me a lot of cider and it had made me sleepy, even though I still hadn't managed to sleep. I remembered that my head was aching when Daddy got into bed. I didn't move. I just had to lie there and wait and see what he would do next.

I wanted to push him away, but I felt too weak and too scared. I wanted to scream out with the pain when he touched me. His big hands reached down between my legs.

I sobbed silently. I tried to wedge my thighs together tightly, ramming my kneecaps against one another until they ached, but I could feel Daddy's fingernails scratching my skin, pulling them apart.

He touched me in my private parts. It made me feel dirty and embarrassed.

Why did Daddy want to touch me there if it was a filthy part of my body? His fingernails dug deeply. Everything felt dirty. But the pain was the worst thing. What was causing so much pain? His fingers were clawing at me, digging into me and hurting me. Please stop, Daddy.

It was only a few days later, a week perhaps, that everything changed again. I was lying in bed, wondering as I always seemed to be these days, what Daddy was going to do to me tonight.

I could hear Mammy's muffled voice downstairs, punctuated by regular pauses when she drained her glass or dragged on a cigarette.

I prayed silently that maybe, just this once, she would come to bed before Daddy came home from the pub and protect me. Deep down, though, I knew that wouldn't happen. I wasn't sure if Mammy knew what Daddy did in bed, but I knew for sure that she never protected me or did anything nice for me at all.

The steady rhythm of her voice and the distant strains of country and western music on the radio went on for what seemed like hours. She wasn't coming to bed any time soon.

I tried to calm myself down. Maybe the things Daddy did

to me were all part of growing up after all. But I just wanted to be like all my other friends.

They all seemed so happy and normal compared to me, but I just knew I could never be normal. I'd already worked out not to hope for things to get better, because they just got worse. There was no point kidding myself. I couldn't imagine ever being happy. I was used to being beaten and insulted, used to Mammy's casual slaps and kicks for no reason and I never knew what I had done to deserve it. I had stopped trying to work it out.

I was dragged out of my thoughts by the familiar sound of Daddy's key in the door. My stomach lurched. I tried to wrap myself in the thick, smelly blanket, hugging it tight around me.

It stank of smoke and scratched my face, but it was my only protection. Maybe Daddy would leave me alone if he saw I was tucked up snugly, asleep? It was worth a try. Anything was worth a try.

I clamped my eyes shut, so hard that I had dark shapes swimming around in front of them and they ached. But no amount of pretence was going to save me; as soon as I heard his footsteps, one by one on the stairs, I knew tonight would be like every other night. He hadn't stopped to speak to Mammy, which could be good or could be bad. There was never any way of telling.

As each step got louder, his old leather shoes slapping on the thin grey lino, my heart beat louder inside my chest. I thought I would explode.

Now I could feel him next to the bed, breathing heavily as he took off his clothes.

I heard that clink of his belt buckle as it hit the floor and then he got into bed behind me, snatching my blanket roughly off me and tossing it over us both.

A cold blast of air whipped across my curled-up body and I shuddered, still trying to pretend to be deep in sleep even though my body was rigid with terror and he was trying to unfold me.

I felt the heat of Daddy's breath on the back of my neck as he pulled himself in close behind me, and the familiar stench of stale beer and pungent sweat started to suffocate me.

I knew something horrible was about to happen, and a little voice inside my head started screaming as my breathing got quicker with fear. Next I felt Daddy's clammy hands clamp around my stomach. I held my breath as he wrenched me back sharply towards him.

Suddenly the pain was so excruciating I almost passed out. My body felt like it was being slit open with a razor-sharp knife.

'No, Daddy, no! Please, Daddy, no!' I stuttered.

It was the first time I had ever broken the silence while he was touching me, but he didn't seem to hear me, and he didn't stop. It was like I wasn't actually there.

I didn't know what he was doing to cause me so much pain – why would I? My head felt foggy, as if I was only half conscious, and the pain was now so bad I thought this must be what it is like just before you die.

'No, Daddy, no! Please, Daddy, no. Please stop,' I begged, whimpering like a wounded animal.

He carried on in silence, getting rougher.

The pain was worse than anything I had experienced in my life before, and then a wave of sickness and panic washed over me as my eight-year-old brain worked out what was causing it.

He was inside me! I could feel him moving backwards and forwards, backwards and forwards. I realized he had entered my back passage. I froze.

He held my thin body tight and kept stabbing and stabbing at me. My bottom burned and the pain shot up through my whole body, right up from my toes to my eyelashes. My head was throbbing. Eventually he shoved me away from him, like I was a rag doll. I held my breath, not daring to move until he fell asleep. Finally, I heard his snores, and tried to muffle the sound of my choking tears, careful not to wake him in case it started all over again.

Chapter 7

Christmas

Christmas was coming.

Daddy's friends gave him big pieces of ham, a turkey and bundles of coal to bring home. There was so much beer and sherry and cider stacked up in the kitchen you could hardly move.

'This is for your mammy!' the men said when they brought their deliveries to the back door.

The house felt warmer than usual. We had tinsel round the picture frames and cards on the mantelpiece, and whenever I heard Mammy whispering I hoped it was all about the presents we might get, rather than secrets we had to keep. I wondered if Christmas might change things, but I didn't really believe it.

Daddy slept in the bed with me every night now. I'd given up trying to imagine it might be part of growing up that would end any day soon, and I certainly didn't think it was any sort of privilege or special treatment any more, because he hurt me so very much. It felt so wrong. And I couldn't tell anybody about it, because I wasn't sure what to say and I didn't want to get into any more trouble. I didn't want Mammy to shout or hit me. I didn't want her to fight with Daddy any more than she already did, so I didn't say a word.

I dreaded going to bed more than ever. Every step I took up the stairs each night felt like a step towards a cold, dark dungeon. What torture would there be tonight? How much would it hurt? Or would Daddy leave me alone? Maybe he would go to sleep, and when we woke up the next day the nightmare would have all ended. But I didn't hold out much hope.

One night, after an evening carol service at school, Mammy gave me more cider than usual. 'Go on, Cynthia, drink the whole tumbler down! It'll help you sleep!' I'd been complaining about my itchy head and the bites on my arms and legs. I'd told Mammy I had trouble sleeping because the itching kept me awake. I wanted her to know I couldn't sleep, but I couldn't tell her the main reason, the big reason.

I forced the icy cider down my throat even though the sharp taste made me want to spit it all out the second it touched my tongue. Only the thought that it would help me sleep, just like Mammy said, made me swallow it. I wanted to sleep. I felt very tired, and the nuns at school were forever telling me off for not concentrating.

I got into bed that night with my head feeling thick and

fuzzy. It was aching inside and itching on the outside. I tried to tell myself tonight would be a good night. Daddy would go to sleep and not touch me. I would fall asleep soon, once I'd heard his long, slow breaths, and I would wake up in the morning feeling grand. I wouldn't be exhausted like I normally was. I wouldn't have black rings under my eyes and a sore head. And I wouldn't be in pain.

My tricks didn't work. My body didn't listen to my head. Lying in bed, I started to tremble and quiver like I always did. My heart started hammering, and I instinctively pressed my legs together, hoping Daddy would leave me alone.

I heard his footsteps. Was he staggering around? Had he drunk lots of beer? It didn't matter. It didn't make any difference. If he wanted to touch me and hurt me he would, I knew that. It wouldn't matter if he was laughing and joking or shouting and cursing when he came in. It didn't give me a clue about what he was going to do once he was in bed with me.

He was in the house now. He had ignored Mammy. She was knitting by the fire and watching a show on the telly. He was on the stairs. I felt so frightened I wondered if I should I jump out of bed and scream for help. No, how could I? All hell would break loose. I'd be beaten severely. Mammy and Daddy would go mad if I woke the little ones up, and they were fast asleep in the cot in the same room, as usual. I wished I could sleep like them.

I had no choice but to lie there and let Daddy do what he

wanted to do. But how could I stand the pain? He hurt me so much. I didn't want to be hurt. Why couldn't Daddy just go to sleep? Please, God, please make him go to sleep tonight. I pressed my hands together in a prayer position. 'Please, God, please! Hear me tonight. Make him go straight to sleep tonight!'

A foul smell descended on the bed as Daddy used the toilet bucket. The thick air felt like an extra blanket, so heavy and suffocating on top of me. The cider in my belly felt as if it was burning a hole in my stomach, and I wished I could vomit to get rid the foul stench catching in my mouth. But it was too late to move or do anything.

Daddy was in bed. He was naked, and he was pushing himself into me and turning me towards him. This wasn't going to be that thing with my mouth, was it? I couldn't stand it.

No, I could feel him hovering over me now. I was afraid he might fall and crush me, and I held my breath, petrified of the pain I knew was coming.

His face was right in front of mine. I stared into his eyes, looking for a flicker of light. Could he see my terrified eyes? Could he see my face, frozen with fear? I was too afraid to speak. It felt like my tongue was glued to the bottom of my mouth. I could hardly breathe. I didn't want to breathe. I didn't want to smell his foul smell. I wanted to spit out his smell, not breathe it in, but I was trapped and paralysed.

I felt like the little bird I'd seen in the garden when the neighbour's cat caught it in its jaws. It seemed to give up the second the cat's jaw locked, like it knew struggling would only make things worse and prolong the agony.

Daddy was doing something different tonight. I felt the clawing down below that I'd felt before, and I screamed inside my head: Not there again. Please don't hurt me down below. Daddy carried on scratching and pushing into me, and then I felt him lower himself on top of me again. It felt dangerous, like he was crushing the breath out of me.

I was so afraid of what he might do next. I thought he might kill me, and I didn't want to die in pain. 'Please stop, Daddy!' I gasped desperately. 'Please, no.'

It was too late. This time Daddy really was killing me. I was going to die, I was sure of it. He was inside me again. I could feel him moving like I had before, but I didn't want to believe it was happening.

I couldn't take it in. It was different to last time. It was even worse. The pain wasn't in my bottom, it was right between my legs.

It wasn't like a knife slitting me open this time. It was ten times worse, like my bones were being ripped apart and then I was being stabbed and stabbed.

I was burning inside, and the pain was shooting right though my tummy and chest and heart and head. I could feel it in my fingertips and eyelids, in my little toes and in my throat. The pain was everywhere, the agony unbearable. I thought I was going to be torn in half and die in two pieces, wrenched apart. 'Please,' was all I had the strength to gasp. I thought I might pass out. It felt like the life was being punched out of me.

Daddy's hard voice cut through the air like a knife. 'It's your ma's fault I have to do these things to you,' he said coldly, without looking at my face.

I gasped in shock. Daddy could hear my pleas! He knew he was hurting me very badly. He was almost killing me with pain. But he didn't stop. He was making excuses!

'It's all her fault because she won't let me do it to her.'

What did he mean? Why would he do this to Mammy? Why would he want to hurt anyone in this horrible way? Should I tell Mammy what he was doing and what he said? My head just swam. Nothing made sense. 'Go down and tell her what I'm doing to you. It's all her fault!'

I was so sore, all my energies went into coping with the pain. I couldn't think straight. Maybe he wanted me to tell Mammy what he said, but I didn't trust him. How could I trust him after he had hurt me so badly? Was it a trap? Mammy might thump me and beat me, and I couldn't bear the thought of any more pain. I wouldn't tell Mammy, if that's what Daddy wanted. I would do what Daddy wanted after he had hurt me so much.

After what felt like ages, Daddy shoved himself as far away from me as possible. Did he hate me so much that he didn't want me near him? I felt hurt by that, even though I didn't want him to touch me ever again. I couldn't understand why he got so close, far too close, if all of a sudden he didn't want me near him. Nothing made sense.

Eventually the burning in my body subsided into numbness, like I'd been beaten black and blue inside and out. No, I couldn't tell anyone at all. I definitely couldn't risk another beating. Another beating would kill me, I was sure of it. I had to be extra good. I had to help Mammy and keep the peace. I had to keep this secret.

Besides, Christmas was coming. Christmas might make things better. Remember that time Daddy took me to Woolworth's and I got a mug of milk and a pink wafer biscuit?

Perhaps this Christmas would be the best ever, the start of good things. We had lots of drink and cigarettes, so Mammy would be happy. I looked at Daddy sleeping on the edge of the bed. I was pressed against the wall. I didn't want to wake Daddy. I didn't want to annoy him in any way. Tomorrow would be better. Tomorrow had to be better. It just couldn't be worse.

About three weeks before Christmas, Daddy surprised me by telling me to pick out what I wanted for my present. Mammy and Daddy gave us separate presents, and Daddy usually let us choose what we wanted.

I'd already spotted a miniature blue piano and a matching stool in a shop window in the main street. My heart melted when I saw it. It was the same baby blue as the old cot, and it had fancy carvings on the legs.

I never thought for a moment I might actually be able to own it, but now Daddy had told me to pick my present I shot straight down to the shop and told the woman behind the counter, 'I'm havin' that! It's mine! Don't sell it to anyone else!'

She looked me up and down and reluctantly agreed, but told me to come back soon. 'I can't keep it for ever, you know. Tell your da he needs to pay for it real soon!'

On my way to the shop I had convinced myself that if Daddy really did buy it for me, it would mean he loved me and the bad things would end.

I couldn't wait to get the money off him, to prove he loved me and that life was going to change. Daddies who bought their little girls beautiful Christmas presents had to love them and care for them, didn't they? Wouldn't I look just the one, playing the piano! Maybe Mammy would even sing along while I played it. I didn't have a clue how to play, but it didn't matter. I had to have it.

I ran straight out of the Golden Gift shop and went racing round the pubs looking for Daddy. I went in about three smoky lounges, my eyes stinging as they scanned the room looking for his Brylcreemed hair or his tweed jacket with the scuffed leather patches on the elbows.

I went in the Club, Hogans and the Queens. 'Are you lookin' for your da, Cynthia love? He hasn't been in here tonight,' a succession of men told me. I felt so out of place in those bars.

Every man in the room seemed to turn his gaze to me when I edged in the door. They frightened me, these smoke-breathing giants.

Where was my Daddy? I needed the money. I needed that piano, I really did.

When I finally found him, in McDonagh's, I could have cried with relief. 'Daddy, Daddy! I've found it! I've picked out my present. I need the money now to pay for it...'

He didn't smile. In fact, I thought he looked as if he might try to hit me, and I held my arms in close to my side and took a step away from him, bracing myself to duck.

'Not now, you'll have to wait another week,' he scowled. I cried all the way home, but I wasn't giving up that easily.

The same ritual went on every week for three weeks. Those smoky giants in the pubs didn't bother me in the end. I'd have fought through flame-breathing dragons to find my daddy and get him to give me the money for my piano.

On Christmas Eve, I finally found him in the Arches, at about quarter to five. When I told him how much money I needed he reacted as if it was the first time he had heard the news. He banged down his pint angrily and said, 'No way – d'you think I'm made of money? It's way too much. No chance! What are you thinking of?'

I felt like crying, but I bit my lip and looked at the floor, wondering what to do now. Maybe if I cried Daddy would give me the money to get rid of me! Now that was a great idea. I had to try it.

I started to snivel pathetically, looking at him with big, sad eyes, and letting the tears trickle dramatically down my cheeks.

'Shut up, you're shaming me,' he snapped.

That was the idea, and my plan worked a treat. One of the men in the pub heard the commotion and said, 'For God's sake, Peter, it's Christmas Eve, give the girl what she wants.'

Daddy grunted and scowled again, took a long slow slug of beer, put his hand in his pocket and gave me the money.

I raced to the shop like my life depended on it and bought my present. 'Take that upstairs,' Mammy tutted when I fell in the back door with it, panting with the effort of carrying the big box home as much as from the euphoria of winning my prize.

But what a prize it was. It told me Daddy loved me, and he wasn't going to hurt me any more.

The piano was placed unwrapped at the end of my bed, which is what Mammy and Daddy told us to do with our gifts every year. I don't remember getting a wrapped present, or a surprise present ever, apart from the little trike that time.

Daddy didn't touch me in bed that night, and for once I fell asleep without trembling with fear. My plan had worked.

Christmas morning was magical. Mammy had prepared all the Christmas dinner the day before, so she could have a lie-in. The house was filled with the smell of turkey and stuffing and roast potatoes. The fire was roaring, and my brothers and sisters were happy and smiling.

I sat myself down at my piano feeling like the cat who'd got the cream. It made a great tinkling sound, and each note I bashed out made me happier and happier.

Yes! Daddy bought it for me! He won't hurt me now, I told

myself over and over again as I sang along, belting out one of Daddy's favourite songs, 'Scarlet Ribbons'. What I liked about that song was the idea that one day I might have scarlet ribbons for my own hair.

Daddy was still in bed when we had our dinner, and I offered to take his food upstairs.

'Sit on the bed and wait till I've finished eating,' he said quietly when I carried the plate to him.

I happily obeyed. The daddy who scared me had gone. He had disappeared in the night, and now I had a daddy who bought me a special present and wanted to spend time with me on Christmas Day.

I watched him start to eat his turkey and all the trimmings. 'Did you like the dinner, Daddy? Did you hear me play my piano? Isn't this the best day ever?'

Daddy was too busy eating to talk to me, but he looked quite calm and relaxed. When he finished eating he put his knife and fork down tidily on the plate and put it on the chest of drawers nearby.

'Move closer to me,' he ordered suddenly. 'Come over to me.'

The way he said it made goosebumps bubble up all over my skin. He wasn't smiling. It was like his face had turned to stone.

The hairs on the back of my neck stood up now. I knew what he wanted, and I couldn't move. I sat there like a little statue, feeling sick and scared and horribly confused.

'Move now! Get here now!' he shouted. His voice was so fierce and angry it triggered me into action. I moved closer to him, and I felt my body start to tremble as he pulled me across his lap.

I tried to shut my eyes so tight it would make everything numb and black, but it didn't work.

I felt a rubbing and pushing up my back and my bottom. My face was pushed down into the blankets but I could hear the kids downstairs laughing and chattering as they played with their presents.

Mary was only small and she'd chosen a plastic doll as her gift. She was thrilled with it, and I tried to picture her happily playing with it to take my mind off what Daddy was doing to me in the bed.

I thought about the Apache Indian doll Mammy had bought me. I loved cowboys and Indians films, and she'd let me pick out this doll with an embroidered face, leather clothes and threaded plaits.

Suddenly the images of the presents and the smiling children and the tinsel downstairs vanished.

That agonizing shooting pain I had felt before had taken over my mind and body again.

I was paralysed by it, and by the fear. I was going to break in two. The smell of the turkey hovered over the bed. I wanted to be sick. Daddy had spoilt Christmas. I thought he loved me. I still wanted him to love me. But he couldn't love me that much if he hurt me and frightened me like this, could he?

I tried not to cry when I put my clothes back on and struggled downstairs. Mary was giggling and giving her dolly a hug. I didn't want to spoil her day, so I sat on the sofa quietly watching, shuffling nervously on my sore bottom.

It felt as if the front bedroom belonged to another world. It was like I'd just stepped out of a scary film and walked back into real life. But real life was scary too. I could still feel the acute pain, even though my heart felt cold and dead.

Mammy glared at me. I'd forgotten to bring the plate back down, and I thought for a second she was going to order me back upstairs to get it. I looked back at her, tears welling up in my eyes, but she just looked away.

She couldn't know what Daddy had just done, could she? Maybe I should tell Mammy what Daddy did after all. I couldn't bear the thought of being hurt that way again. It had to stop, but what could I say, and how would Mammy react? I had no idea, but I knew I had to try.

Chapter 8

Telling Mammy

I loved New Year's Eve. It was my favourite time of year. All the boats out at sea would sound their foghorns at midnight and the church bells would ring in the New Year.

We called it the Boats and the Bells, and when I was smaller I remembered Mammy would tell me to hurry up and go to sleep so that she could wake me up at midnight to hear the celebrations. Then I was allowed to run outside and wish the neighbours a Happy New Year.

This year, I didn't feel excited at all. I was only eight-years-old, but nothing seemed to make me feel excited any more. When Granny called round to tell me one of her stories it cheered me up, but not much.

Even my blue piano didn't make me happy. I looked at it stowed in the corner, untouched for days. It had a layer of dust on it already. I didn't want to play it, and I didn't want to sing. What Daddy did on Christmas Day made me so very sad.

123

My head hurt all the time. I had asked Mammy for pills the night before it was so bad, but she shouted at me. 'No, Cynthia, I might have a hangover tomorrow! You can't have my painkillers.' The foghorns sounded out as noisily as ever when midnight struck, but my own head felt so foggy the booming sound didn't inspire me like it normally did. It was just a noise in the distance, another sound bouncing aimlessly around in my head.

'What's your New Year's resolution going to be this year, Cynthia?' asked one of our neighbours in the street.

All the other kids were chattering and shouting out their resolutions, like learning to swim, doing their homework or helping their mammy make bread.

I had so many things I wanted to change in my life, I didn't know where to start. 'I don't know – wash the dishes for Mammy!' I offered, while inside I thought: Tell Mammy. Pluck up the courage to tell Mammy what Daddy does in bed. Ever since Christmas Day I had been trying to be brave enough to tell her how much he hurt me, but I was terrified. I thought back to when Mammy called me a 'dirty bastard' for walking in on her getting dressed. She had just been in her bra, and she looked ashamed and tried to cover herself up. Would she think I was dirty? When Mother Dorothy had told me off for wearing smelly knickers Mammy had screamed, 'Don't go talking about the filthy parts of your body! I'll wash your mouth out with soap and water, you filthy little bitch!'

I looked at the other kids, making up their resolutions like

124

I used to. I had to tell Mammy, I just had to. I didn't want to be sore and in pain. I wanted to have fun and be happy and normal like other kids. I had to see if it was possible. I had to tell.

I spent many weeks agonizing over it. There was nobody else I could talk to. I couldn't tell my friends. It would be too embarrassing. What if it was normal and I was making a big fuss about something everybody did? What if *I* wasn't normal? What could they do to help?

I definitely couldn't tell Mother Dorothy. I didn't know if what Daddy did was sinful, but I felt dirty afterwards. It felt wrong. I thought that Mother Dorothy would beat me for being dirty, or tell me I was a liar and a sinner. Being caned with Mr Greeny was the last thing I wanted. And what if she confronted Daddy? Having a nun knocking on our door to talk to him about it was unthinkable; that would bring me untold misery. There was Granny, I suppose, but I wanted to be happy with Granny. She was my escape. I couldn't tell her. What if she told Mammy? She'd have a fit about me talking about what went on in our house behind her back.

Daddy had started to hurt me in the mornings sometimes too, especially Sunday mornings when Mammy was still fast asleep. One Sunday morning, he was pushing himself on me in the single bed, while Mammy lay across the room in the double bed. I didn't struggle, because I had learned that it hurt more if I did.

I was tracing my finger along a curved pattern on the faded

Cynthia Owen

wallpaper to focus my mind away from what was happening to me, when I suddenly heard Mary and Martin playing at the bottom of the stairs.

They were whispering so as not to wake Mammy and Daddy, because at the weekend the little ones weren't allowed downstairs alone when Mammy and Daddy were still in bed.

'Give it to me! It's my turn!' I heard one of them hiss.

Suddenly, a thought flashed into my head: If I can hear them at the bottom of the stairs, then perhaps Mammy can hear what Daddy is doing to me on the other side of the room?

The thought made my heart leap with hope. It meant Mammy could find out what was happening without me having to find the words to tell her.

I let out some of my stifled sobs one by one, and I turned my head and watched Mammy closely. She stirred a little. I saw her eyelids flicker, and I was sure she was awake.

I kept watching her intently, looking at every little movement she made. My legs and my back ached. It was agony between my legs, but I didn't struggle. I let Daddy carry on hurting me, and all the time I was willing Mammy to wake up and see what he was doing. Please, Mammy! Please wake up, a little voice in my head screamed. Please hear him. Please stop him!

My eyes bored into her face. She stirred again, and her breathing wasn't like the normal long, slow pants she made when she was deep in sleep. It sounded like her daytime breathing. She had to be awake.

She stirred again, then I watched in horror as she pulled her blanket over her face and turned her back on me, her eyes clamped shut.

My mind raced: 'She's awake and she knows what he's doing! She knows I'm crying in pain, but she's letting him do it. It must be normal! She's awake, and she knows what he's doing!'

But maybe I had imagined she was awake. Maybe she heard nothing and saw nothing. Afterwards, Daddy sent me to the shop to buy the Sunday papers.

My thighs were stinging as I walked through the main street in the village. It was a beautiful sunny day, birds were singing in the sky and families were out together going to and from mass.

As I turned a corner I felt a trickle of wetness fill my knickers. It was the horrible stuff Daddy put in my hair sometimes, and round my mouth. I felt so very dirty, and so very confused.

I looked at the other little children, chatting and smiling, and I wondered how they could look so happy after their daddies had just done what my daddy had done. Weren't they in pain? Didn't they feel dirty to have wet knickers and a stinging bottom? How could they smile?

I didn't have any answers, and in time I decided I had to go through with my New Year's resolution. However risky it was, I had to speak to Mammy. I had to pluck up the courage to talk to her and tell her how sad I felt, and how sore I was. I had to do something, because I couldn't think of anything else. It was mixing round in my brain all the time, taking all my energy and making me feel ill.

Mother Dorothy was giving out steam to me all the time too. One Monday morning, I couldn't concentrate at all. My brain felt fuzzy. When Mother Dorothy asked me a simple sum I got it wrong. I hid in the toilet at break time fretting, wondering if I was going mad.

I just needed five minutes to think and gather my head together, but the door banged moments later. It was the thud of Mr Greeny!

'Come out of there!' Mother Dorothy bellowed.

I slunk out of the cubicle. 'Sorry, Mother Dorothy, it won't happen again,' I said, not knowing quite what I was apologizing for. I was going crazy. I had to talk to Mammy.

A few days later, Mammy was standing alone in the kitchen, scrubbing carrots. This was my moment. I just had to spit it out, and then Mammy would help me and I wouldn't go mad, I was sure of it. She called me nasty names and she lost her temper and gave me plenty of beatings, but she wouldn't want me to suffer this badly, would she? She was my mammy, and she wouldn't want Daddy to hurt me so much I thought I was going to die. I didn't know why Daddy did it, but maybe Mammy could help explain things?

Horrible doubts still wriggled around in my head about how she would react. What if she called me a dirty bitch, or even hit me?

But then, how hard could she hit me? I was sure none of

Mammy's punches and slaps could hurt me as much as Daddy hurt me. I had to tell her. I was desperate for the the agony to end.

'Mammy...' I stuttered. 'I have something to tell you.' She ignored me and carried on scrubbing the carrots by the sink, which was overflowing with dirty dishes. I noticed her fingers were red raw, and a cigarette was hanging out of her mouth. She didn't look happy, but I had to get this over with.

'Mammy, can I tell you something?'

'What is it now? Can't you see I've enough to do? That dirty bastard of a father of yours has pissed all over the pots again. Fuckin' filthy bastard.'

'Mammy... I don't like what Daddy does.'

'What? Nor do I! Useless bastard!'

'No, Mammy, I mean I don't like what Daddy does to me.'

'What? You're talking nonsense, Cynthia. What Daddy does to you when? I don't like what your da does most of the fuckin' time.'

'Mammy, I don't like what Daddy does in bed.' I could feel my cheeks burning, just like they had done when Mother Dorothy hauled me to the front of the class and pointed out the lice in my hair. It was so humiliating. I hoped Mammy didn't ask me to say any more.

'Now what are you talking about, Cynthia?' she moaned, rolling her eyes and scrubbing faster at the carrots.

'I don't like it when he gets too close...when he...touches me.'

She dragged on her cigarette, and some ash fell into the sink. I watched it dissolve in the dirty dishwater, and I felt as if some of my stress and suffering had melted away too. I'd said it. I'd actually told Mammy.

She said nothing for a moment, and I looked at her face expectantly. Her green eyes were as cold as marbles. 'Oh come on, Cynthia, it's all in your imagination,' she blurted out. 'It's just your father moving around in the bed because he's drunk!' She turned her back on me and went to fetch something from the far end of the kitchen.

I stumbled into the living room and slumped onto the sofa. I felt like I'd been crushed. My ray of hope had gone. It was as if I was slowly dying from the inside. Mammy wasn't going to help me. I was all on my own, and I felt so terribly lonely.

My mind went back to that Sunday morning when she was lying in the double bed on the other side of the front room. My instincts had been right. She had been awake, and she did know what he was doing. She had deliberately turned her back on me, just like she had done at the sink just now.

My mind was churning again. Was it because what Daddy did was normal? Maybe. But even if it was normal, now she knew I didn't like it and I wanted it to stop, why didn't she help me?

For some reason she didn't want to stop it. She didn't want to help me. She didn't even want to talk about it. I was devastated.

That night, I climbed into bed feeling more terrified than

ever. There was simply no escape. Even if I ran screaming from the bed when Daddy got in, Mammy would send me back and tell me not to be such a silly bitch. I knew that now, so what could I do?

A great idea came to me as I trembled in the dark. What if I lay with my head at the opposite end of the bed? It would be harder for Daddy to reach me, and maybe he would give up and leave me alone.

I was shaking so much I could hardly shuffle down the bed. I curled into the tiniest ball possible and pressed myself against the wall, hoping maybe he wouldn't even see me. I clung on to that thought for hours as I lay there shivering, waiting for him to come home.

The key in the lock startled me as usual, but I was sure my plan would work. It was a fine plan. Daddy would leave me alone. He might not even see me!

Moments later, I felt the mattress ripple as Daddy got under the bedclothes. A wave of cold air swept over me. I was curled up so tightly I could feel my own hot breath on my chest and fingertips, as I had my hands balled up in front of my face like a little mouse.

Something sharp dug into my leg. It was Daddy's toenail spiking in my shin. I felt it dig in again. It wasn't an accident. He was kicking me hard.

'Get here now!' he growled. I couldn't move. I was too scared, but he was still kicking me, and there was a strange pulsating feeling in my legs.

'Get here now!' He sounded even scarier this time, and the fear jolted me to my knees. I crawled to the top of the bed, crying and struggling.

Daddy's arms felt like they were all over me. He was trying to unfold me and turn me around to face him, but I didn't want to look at him. I kept myself rigid and curled up, shaking my head and saying, 'No, Daddy. Please, Daddy, no!' I felt his grip on my arms loosen, and the mattress rippled again. He was out of the bed!

I panted for air. I could breathe again. I could hardly believe it. I'd got rid of him, but I didn't dare move. Seconds later, I heard his belt buckle clink and the sound made me catch my breath again. Surely he wasn't going to beat me? No, one thing was certain: he never beat any of us kids in our beds.

I felt the cold leather across my chest now, but he hadn't hit me. It was tar black in the room and I couldn't make out what was happening. What was he going to do with the belt if he wasn't going to beat me?

Next I felt the leather shift across my back, and then the buckle tighten on my chest. He had tied his belt around my arms and chest.

'Try struggling now!' he snarled, climbing on to me and hurting my whole body. As always, the pain was unbearable, but I had to endure it. There seemed no way out. It seemed worse than ever, because I was tied up like a prisoner. I cried myself to sleep after many hours. He left me tied up all night, and in the morning the buckle had left a deep imprint in my chest, reminding me of the horrors of the night before. I struggled and wriggled free when he undid it, but inside I still felt like a prisoner.

During the daytime, whatever the day brought, it felt as if everything I did was spoilt by memories that flashed in my head, reminding me what Daddy did in bed. He frightened me and hurt me so much I couldn't ever stop thinking about it or worrying about what was to come.

I had always loved escaping from the house to play on the street, yet everything I did felt tainted.

The boys mostly played football, but sometimes we would all hold hands in a circle and play 'The farmer wants a wife,' 'Little Sally saucer' or 'Ring a ring a rosie'.

We played skipping-rope games too, like 'I'm a little girl guide all dressed in blue', using a rope begged off our neighbour. It was such a happy-go-lucky song, but how could I sing like I didn't have a care in the world? I was sore and scared. I had an itchy head and dirty nails and scruffy clothes. I'd love to be a little girl guide all dressed in blue, but I knew I never would be. I was Daddy's slave, and that was all I was ever going to be.

The egg man called every week and told us the eggs could talk. I'd be in stitches as he put on silly voices and made the eggs dance around, saying: 'Good day to you! How are you this fine day?' I wished Daddy would make me laugh like that, but he never did. He just made me cry.

Once the rag-and-bone man came down the street on his

horse and cart shouting, 'Any old rags, any old rags!' like he always did.

In exchange for bits of old cloth and materials he would give us a brightly coloured balloon. Normally, I had nothing for him, but I hated Daddy so much that day I gave the rag-and-bone man one of his best shirts, in return for three huge balloons.

I didn't care if I got a beating. Nothing could hurt me as much as Daddy hurt me in bed, or as much as Mammy hurt me by ignoring what was going on. I might as well have a bit of fun, and for a few minutes I did, as I ran down the street with my three red balloons dancing behind me. Moments like that stopped me going mad, I was sure.

My ninth birthday was coming up, but I didn't expect it to be special. Martin's birthday was just a couple of months before mine, and Mammy had sent me to the Golden Gift shop in the village to buy him a yellow truck and a big card. 'Martin's my favourite child,' she told me. 'Make sure you get a great big card!'

'It's my birthday next week,' I informed Mammy one afternoon. I knew it was in October. I'd remembered from the year before.

'No it isn't,' snapped Mammy, without looking up at me. She was making the beds, and it had become her routine to ask me to help her make them in the afternoons, after Granny had called round for a cup of tea at 4 p.m.

'You're wrong. You're lying,' she snarled.

I knew Daddy kept all the birth certificates downstairs in a box in the dresser. I wasn't going to let Mammy get away with this. She didn't have a clue about dates, because she couldn't read or write, and we had no calendar or diary, but I ran downstairs defiantly and pulled the box out. I found my certificate at the bottom of the pile, and I was right. It was my birthday next week.

'See, Mammy, I wasn't lying! It is my birthday! Can I have a present like Martin...'

She didn't answer me, and so I carried on poking my nose around in the dresser. Mammy kept her photo album in there, and she looked through the pictures quite often, adding little keepsakes. She liked to keep a lock of hair from dead relatives and weird things like that.

I leafed through the book quickly, in case Mammy went mad if she saw me. The album fell open on a photograph of me and Esther. Mammy had drawn a big red heart around Esther's head, and scrawled a thick black cross over my face.

Mammy walked up behind me and made me jump. 'Why have you done that, Mammy?' I asked nervously. I wasn't really that shocked, because Mammy had told me lots of times I was her least favourite child, but it still hurt me deeply.

'I did that because you're an evil bitch, Cynthia Murphy! You've got the devil in you – didn't you know?' she taunted.

I didn't react. I'd heard it all before. I simply showed her the birth certificate and told her I was right about my birthday. 'Look, I didn't lie. Please can I have a present?'

'No,' she barked, 'you cannot! Nosy little bitch. Here's a few shillings to get yourself a card, but that's your lot. Bring me back every scrap of change.'

I raced to the shop, glad to escape, and picked out the prettiest and most expensive card I could afford.

When I got home Mammy held out her hand for the scraps of change and told me to write in it myself: 'Happy Birthday to Cynthia.' She'd made me do that before and I never thought too much about it. This time I stared at the words blankly. They meant nothing at all, except how little my mammy thought of me.

Daddy went mad the moment he got home. 'Who's been at the certificate box? Get here, you!'

I was wearing a knee-length skirt and ankle socks, and before I even saw it coming Daddy's leather belt was splitting the skin open on the backs of my legs like they were ripe tomatoes bursting in the sun.

'Please stop! Mammy, tell him to stop,' I panted, scrabbling at the sofa to stop myself hitting the floor. Mammy just laughed.

'Why should I?' she asked coldly, watching with her arms folded as Daddy shoved me to the ground when he'd finally run out of breath.

I looked at the card above me on the mantelpiece and cried. It wasn't worth it, it really wasn't.

My Confirmation was coming up. It was a huge occasion in every Catholic child's life, but I found it impossible to look forward to it. I never got my hopes up about anything any more.

The Bishop of Dublin was coming to the village. I got new socks and a new dress – the first since my First Holy Communion – but my heart barely fluttered when I tried them on.

My head felt thick and heavy, like it did after I drank the cider. I had nasty thoughts and images invading my mind all the time. In my mind's eye I could see Daddy's black finger-nails. I could see him coming closer to me in bed, and I could see myself wrinkling my nose when I smelled his foul sweat.

The images popped into my head at school and in church, and when I played with my friends in the street. Why did he do that to me? Why did he hurt me so much?

Things always went wrong for me. They always turned bad. I always seemed to end up in tears. It was best not to build up my hopes, so I didn't get excited about my Confirmation.

Peter and I were to be confirmed together. I was pleased about that, because we had to go to the altar in pairs of boys and girls holding hands, and it would be less embarrassing holding hands with my brother than with another boy.

Before I made my Confirmation, I had to take 'the Pledge', which meant I promised hand on heart never to drink alcohol.

I wondered if I should confess to the priest that Mammy already gave me cider, but I immediately thought better of it. Instead, I stuck to the same invented confessions every week, telling fibs about stealing and cursing, and then being chastised by the priest and Mother Dorothy for my fictitious sins. I actually came to enjoy seeing the pair of them explode with rage at my repeated audacity.

It was all very confusing. Mammy and Daddy drank every day, yet they were 'good Catholics'. At least that's what Mammy told me, and they must be because they had a picture of the Pope on the wall and holy statues on the mantelpiece. Drinking alcohol couldn't be that big a sin. Mammy even put whiskey and sherry in the younger kids' bottles to get them to sleep at night.

I took 'the Pledge', then went home to witness Mammy drinking glass after glass of sherry, forcing me to drink cider before she sent me to bed and ranting at my father when he came stumbling in from the pub.

It didn't really make any sense. Grown-ups seemed to live by a separate set of rules to us kids. Maybe now I was getting older I would start to understand their rules more. Maybe that would make my life a bit better? I hoped so but, deep down, again, I didn't really believe it.

Chapter 9

Scarlet Ribbons

I loved it when Granny came round for a cup of tea. She came at 4 p.m., and it was my favourite time of day.

'Mammy, Granny's here! Have you finished makin' the beds?' I shouted up the stairs. Mammy was still in bed, but that was my secret message to her to warn her Granny was here and she needed to come downstairs.

While Mammy threw on her dress and a pair of saggy ankle socks, Granny and I drank hot, sweet tea. Granny had brought me a juicy pear and cut the black bits off for me, and I gobbled it down in three mouthfuls. I sat by her legs and begged her to tell me the story of how the Black and Tans used to knock on her door for a meal. It was one of my favourites and I knew it off by heart, but I got Granny to repeat it.

'Well, Cynthia, the Black and Tans brought me food, and then I would use it to prepare a lavish meal for them,' she explained patiently. 'To tell the truth, the food had probably been stolen from a local store, but I never let on I knew anything about that!'

She leaned her rosy cheeks down towards me, and I could see her blackened teeth as she spoke. 'D'ya know what, Cynthia?' she whispered. 'I hated the Black and Tans, but they always left us plenty of food after those dinners! We were so poor, and our children so hungry, that I would pray to God to send them knocking on our door!'

I laughed and laughed, and when we'd finished our tea I begged Granny to let me walk her home so I could be with her longer. Sometimes she let me come in, and she played me her accordion or showed me how to do an Irish jig.

'Mammy, is it OK if I walk Granny home tonight?' I asked hopefully.

'Not tonight, Cynthia,' Mammy said. 'I need you to help me finish the beds.'

I sighed and felt sad when Granny left. Mammy was already back upstairs.

'Come straight up and help me now, Cynthia,' she shouted. I couldn't tell her mood from her voice, and I felt a bit worried. Was she angry with me? I wasn't sure.

As soon as I walked into the front bedroom, Mammy marched over to the bed I often shared with Daddy and pulled the bedclothes off in a fury. My heart sank. She was in a bad mood, and I was about to find out why.

Her eyes were flashing, and she was dragging furiously on

a cigarette. I picked up a doll off the floor and started playing with it absentmindedly.

Mammy started talking to herself, saying something about Daddy 'playing with himself'. I didn't know what she meant, and I didn't know whether she wanted me to say something, so I sat on the floor and carried on playing with my doll, keeping my head bowed.

'Dirty bastard!' she complained. 'Playing with himself!'

What could she mean? I never saw Daddy play any games. He never played with me, so what game was he playing with himself? I didn't dare ask.

'Can't you hear me, Cynthia? Can't you hear what I'm saying?'

'Yes, Mammy,' I muttered.

'Your father's a dirty bastard. He's playing with himself, didn't you hear what I said?'

'I don't understand, Mammy. Are you cross because he's playing by himself and he doesn't play with us?'

'No, Cynthia, not playing by himself, playing WITH himself.'

She was absolutely furious now. She threw a pile of bedclothes on the floor and started moving her hand up and down dramatically in front of her private parts, to act out what she meant. It reminded me of the way Daddy made me rub him up and down on his private parts, but surely Mammy wasn't talking about that? I felt hot and embarrassed.

'Why would he do that?' I asked, totally at sea.

'To make stuff come out of him!' she screeched. I was

getting frightened now. 'Come and look! Come and look at the sheets!' I trailed to the bed, the doll dangling by one arm at my side, and dutifully looked at the pale stain on the grey sheet. There was blood on the sheet too, and I realized it was my blood, because Daddy hurt me so much sometimes I bled.

I didn't know what to say. Mammy was livid. She was spitting when she spoke, just like Mother Dorothy did when she caned me, and like Daddy had done once when he couldn't get the leather belt buckled across my chest.

I said nothing at all and looked at the floor, waiting for the moment to end. Eventually Mammy wore herself out with her ranting and raving and went downstairs swearing and cursing my father.

The next night, I dreaded the moment Granny said, 'I'll be off now!'

As soon as the words came out of her lips, I shot to my feet and offered to walk her home. 'No, Cynthia,' Mammy glared. 'You're to help me with the beds again.'

I started to tremble when I walked up the stairs.

This time Mammy searched the bedclothes and seemed to find nothing. 'Where is it?' she said frantically. Then she started rummaging in the chest of drawers by the bed.

'Is it on his shirt? Dirty bastard! What's he done with his dirty shirt?'

I felt very scared of Mammy. While she rummaged and cursed, her eyes darted around wildly and her red hair shot out around her like wildfire.

'I don't know, Mammy,' I said, whenever I thought one of her questions was directed at me. I just wanted this to stop.

This frightening routine went on for many weeks. I started to see that if Mammy couldn't find a stain on the sheets, that was the worst possible thing. She went mad and started clawing through all of Daddy's shirts saying, 'I'll find it! Dirty bastard!' Whenever she did find a stain, it calmed her immediately.

But on one occasion she found no stain at all, anywhere. 'What's going on?' she demanded of me. I sat wide-eyed on the floor, picking at my feet nervously.

I thought back to the night before. Was she asking me if Daddy had made a stain in bed last night? How could I answer? When I told her I didn't like what Daddy did in bed she told me it was all in my imagination, he was just rolling over drunk, so what could I say? What did she want me to say? A horrible wave of panic crept over me. Was she cross that Daddy hadn't touched me last night?

Suddenly Mammy was standing over me. My mind panicked and whirled so much, little black patches appeared in front of my eyes. Something was happening I really didn't like.

I was on the bed now. I had clothes on the top half of my body, but my skirt and knickers had gone. What was happening? I was trembling. What was Mammy doing? What was she looking for?

Her head was between my legs. I looked at her face in

horror. There were deep, angry frown lines etched into her forehead.

I let out a shrill cry. Mammy was biting me in between my legs. 'Mammy, please…'

'Shut up, you little bitch!'

'But Mammy I don't like it.'

She carried on, gnawing at me. I wanted to shrivel up and die. Not Mammy as well. I started to struggle and begged her to stop, but Mammy gripped my hips tight with her fingernails, just like Daddy did sometimes.

'Lie still, or I will make it hurt! Lie still or I will bite you!'

When she finally left me alone, I tried to get my brain working again. It felt thick and clouded, like it usually did these days. But I thought I had worked it out. If she thought Daddy hadn't done anything to me the night before, she did that the next day.

It went on for a long time. I started to stagger round like a zombie at school. I mucked about with my friends and had a laugh at break time, putting on little shows and singing Beatles songs I'd heard on the radio, but getting through lessons was a struggle.

In the classroom I felt like I was on another planet. I constantly marvelled at how other girls looked so pretty and loved and cared for, and wondered why I couldn't be like them. What had I done to be treated so badly by both my parents? And why did Mother Dorothy give out so much steam to me when it wasn't my fault I was smelly and dirty, and my head always felt so full and sore I couldn't do my work properly?

At home, I tried to keep out of trouble. I wanted to be as invisible as possible and, thankfully, my parents ignored me whenever it suited them.

However, it meant, whenever they did speak to me, it spelt trouble of one sort or another. I dreaded them talking to me.

'Cynthia, you're to come downstairs,' I heard Daddy call. I had been lying awake in bed as usual when I heard him come in, and had been surprised to hear another man's voice downstairs too.

Mammy was chatting away brightly, pouring drinks, and I had fallen asleep not long afterwards, feeling relieved Daddy had a 'friend' over and was downstairs drinking for once instead of upstairs hurting me.

I had grabbed at the chance of sleep, but now Daddy was calling in my ear, leaning over me and rocking my shoulder.

'Come downstairs straight away!' he told me firmly. Daddy seemed quite excited and was pulling me out of the bed. 'Quickly. In your vest and knickers is fine. Don't get dressed,' he ordered.

I wondered what was going on. Normally Mammy never let me back downstairs at night, and it must have been very late, too, if Daddy was in from the pub.

'I want you to sing the song "Scarlet Ribbons",' Daddy said.

I rubbed my sleepy eyes and scampered down the stairs filled with nervous curiosity. I was introduced to the 'friend' in the living room, and immediately noticed he seemed to be licking his lips.

I didn't like that, but I did as I was told and sang the song. I loved singing, and because 'Scarlet Ribbons' was one of Daddy's favourite songs I'd sung it lots of times and knew it well. As soon as I started singing I remembered what had happened at Christmas after I sang it.

I had taken Daddy's dinner upstairs, and then Christmas was ruined. That wouldn't happen tonight though. Daddy had a 'friend' over. Even Mammy was smiling. I sang my heart out, and everyone was beaming.

'The nice man is sleeping here tonight,' Daddy said to me afterwards. 'He is sleeping in your bed – so go and show him where your bed is.'

This took me by surprise, and my heart started beating faster. I didn't want to share my bed with a stranger.

I wondered what would happen in the bed. Was this man just a 'friend' of Daddy's who needed somewhere to sleep, or was something going to happen?

I sat quietly downstairs worrying while the man went out to his car and came back with some cigarettes and a crate of beer, which he handed to Mammy. Then he gave her a large bunch of notes, and climbed the stairs with me.

I pointed to the bed, and the strange man took off his clothes and got in first, in his underwear, on the inside, nearest to the wall.

I really didn't want to get in the bed, but I knew I had to

do what Daddy told me. The man stripped off his underwear and started pointing at his private parts, as if he was suggesting I touch him down below.

He did it in quite a gentle, coaxing way and, although I was horrified, I didn't feel as frightened as when Daddy forced my hand down and made me touch him.

I didn't want to touch this man though, so I shook my head and said, 'No.' He moved closer to me, and I started to panic in case he got rough and aggressive like Daddy. 'No, please! I don't want to!' I stammered, putting my hands over my face.

After a while I heard him get out of bed and go downstairs. I lay wide-eyed now, my stomach in tight little knots as I panicked about what might happen next.

The man returned with Mammy, whose eyes were blazing, even though she was talking calmly. 'Stop being silly and let the nice man do what he wants,' she said.

I felt petrified. What did he want to do to me? Why was Mammy making me do things with this strange man? I just wanted to go to sleep in peace. I was tired and frightened, but Mammy was getting agitated, and that might make things go really bad.

'Just do it, Cynthia!' she ordered crossly. Now the man was kneeling on the bed, and I could see his 'thing'. It scared me to death, and I started to shudder and slam my legs together. I struggled, but Mammy had hold of me and was trying to push me on top of that thing.

'It won't take a minute,' she told me impatiently, but still

Cynthia Owen

I struggled. I knew the pain that lay in store if I sat on him. I couldn't face it.

'I won't hurt you,' the man said.

It did hurt though. I wasn't sure exactly what he did, but my mind went blank and I cried afterwards for a very long time.

As I lay there sobbing and shaking I listened to Mammy and Daddy and his 'friend' talking politely downstairs. It was so strange. Would it always be like this?

The next day at school, I couldn't get the previous night out of my head. I wanted to tell my friend Eileen all about it to try to make some sense of what had happened, but I just knew I shouldn't talk about it. Besides, I would never have found the words.

Esther came back for a visit not long afterwards. I always loved her visits, because she was kind to me and brought me new socks and pencils.

One afternoon, she walked down to the harbour with me and we sat on the beach and chatted like in the old days. I didn't hold her hand any more. I think I was too big for that.

Something Mammy said had stuck in my head. Just before Esther came back for her previous visit, Mammy had lost her temper one day and told me, 'Esther thinks you're a little bitch! She looks down her nose at us all now she's moved away. She couldn't wait to get away!'

'Mammy, that's not true!' I cried. I knew it was a lie, but Mammy was adamant. 'Don't tell Esther anything about what goes on in this house. I'll kill you if you do! She'll look down her nose even more at us if you tell her things. Keep your mouth shut.'

Mammy told me lots of things that weren't true. She was always telling me not to tell, or to shut up and say nothing. She got me to lie to the priest about why we didn't go to church, and she was forever getting me to lie to the nuns at school about why Martin went to school with me in his buggy, or why I hadn't done my homework or brought in the correct equipment.

I was sure this was another lie. I really wanted to talk to Esther and tell her a few things about Mammy, but I felt afraid. What would Mammy do if she found out I had disobeyed her?

I looked out to sea and shuffled uncomfortably on the sand. I watched the waves for ages, letting all my thoughts wash over me. I thought about Mammy threatening to beat me if I told Esther what went on in our house. In the end, I wasn't brave enough to say anything.

Chapter 10

The Relatives

Another one of Mammy's secrets was Uncle Frank. He was married to Mammy's older sister, Aunt Mag, but Daddy hated him. 'That man is not to come near this house!' I had heard him yell one night. 'D'you hear me? He is never to step foot in this house, ever!'

Daddy was furious. He and Mammy had a terrible fight, and I heard Mammy smash something on the floor. It sounded like Daddy whacked her with his fist, and they both screamed and shouted for ages. 'You know what that girl accused him of! I don't want anyone knockin' on my door! Why would we have a man like that in our house? What would the cops think? Answer me that, you stupid cow!' I tried to make sense of it, but I couldn't. What did Daddy mean? I cried into my pillow, hoping the shouting would stop, and wondering what Daddy would do when he came upstairs.

That night seemed to go on for ever. By now, I had stopped

struggling with Daddy when he got in bed, because struggling made him angrier, and he usually hurt me more when he was fuming with rage. I didn't want him to tie me up with the belt, so I lay there rigid with fear, ready to give in and let him do what he wanted to do, just to get it over with as quickly as possible.

When he reached out to grab me, I had to bite my own hand to stifle my sobs. I didn't want to wake the little ones, and I was scared what Mammy might do if I made a row. The pain felt worse than ever, though I didn't know how that was possible. This time it felt like it went on and on, for an hour or more. I thought I would die of exhaustion and agony, and I cried with relief when, at last, Daddy pushed me away from him like a soiled rag.

Uncle Frank came round the next day. When I saw his fat face appear round the living-room door, my heart sank like a stone. Mammy had invited him round while Daddy was out, and I was terrified of what would happen if he found out.

'Go and sit on Uncle Frank's lap!' Mammy ordered me. I looked at him and winced. He was a baker, and had made me a cake for my birthday once, the only birthday cake I'd ever had. I didn't want to be rude, so I sat on his lap.

I noticed dribble running down his chin, and it reminded me of how Daddy's 'friend' had licked his lips when I sang 'Scarlet Ribbons'. Something bad was going to happen. I just knew it. 'Give your Uncle Frank a kiss,' Mammy shouted across at me. 'No,' I said, shaking my head, feeling shy and awkward. I hated being on his flabby lap. It made me feel sick. 'I'll give you ten shillings!' Uncle Frank grinned.

'Go on, Cynthia!' Mammy urged. 'Ten whole shillings! What's the matter with you? Give your Uncle Frank a nice big kiss now.' I wanted to get off his lap, so I went to give him a quick peck, but Uncle Frank's face suddenly seemed to close in.

His sweaty cheeks rubbed against mine, the saliva on his chin was rubbing on my chin, and his wet lips were pushing on to my mouth. I squirmed and tried to gasp for breath, but as I opened my lips Uncle Frank put his tongue inside my mouth. I was shocked by how big and fat and slimy it felt. It was disgusting, and I ran away as soon as his grip on me softened.

I complained to Mammy bitterly afterwards. 'Shut up complainin', Cynthia,' she said. 'You're such an ungrateful bitch. Just do it without moaning next time, and take his money.'

Around this time, I was getting into pop music. My older sisters liked it too, so I didn't have much choice but to listen to what they played. I loved dancing to jive and anything by the Beatles or the Rolling Stones. Sometimes, when Mammy had had plenty to drink, I was allowed to put on records late at night and sing and dance around the room.

On the odd occasion she was in a good enough mood, Mammy sat in her rocking chair by the coal fire watching me, and one night she suggested that I strip off my jumper to cool down, because the fire was blazing and I was rosy-cheeked.

The music was blaring, Mammy was drinking and I was dancing wildly. It was great not to think about anything but the beat of the music for a change. Mammy was laughing, and even clapping in time now and again. The atmosphere was good and I was really enjoying myself for once.

My woollen jumper was cast aside, but I was still burning hot. The fire was roaring fiercely. I hadn't seen that much coal on it since Christmas.

'Take off another layer!' Mammy said, over and over again, until in the end I was dancing in my thin vest.

Then she got up, drew the curtains wide and threw open the window. I hadn't seen her let in any fresh air and light like that for years, and I watched her curiously, feeling a little wary.

Suddenly, I let out a shriek. There was a shadowy face at the window!

'Mammy! There's somebody out there!' I screamed.

She made a huge drama out of going out to investigate, and when she didn't come back for ages, something made me follow her. It wasn't like Mammy to dart about, and she hardly ever went outside. I knew she was up to something.

As I tiptoed out through the back door, I spotted her talking furtively to my Uncle Frank behind the coal shed. She had a bottle of sherry in her hand, and he had a wide smile on his slimy lips.

Had he been outside the whole time I was prancing around in my vest? Was that why Mammy had encouraged me to have fun, dancing around? Was that why she had put so much coal on the fire, so I would be so hot I would have to strip off?

I was seething, and decided I would be brave and tell Daddy when I got the chance. I knew he had banned Uncle Frank from the house. I was going to tell him he had been prowling round in the garden. If Mammy beat me, I would just accept it. It would be a small price to pay to get rid of Uncle Frank once and for all.

I don't know what happened between Mammy and Daddy after I muttered to him nervously one night about Uncle Frank in the garden, but Mammy thumped me on the ear very hard one day without warning.

'Nosy little bitch!' she called me. Every time the pain rang in my ear, which it did for several days, I told myself it was worth it if Uncle Frank was banished from our house for good and I never had to kiss him ever again.

The following Sunday, while Daddy slept in, Mammy came downstairs and announced that Uncle Frank and Aunt Mag had invited me for Sunday dinner at their home.

'Get yourself ready, Cynthia. They'll be here to collect you soon,' Mammy said coldly. 'Be a good girl and do as Uncle Frank asks you, d'you hear?'

My heart sank and my stomach started to knot with nerves.

Mammy rarely let me inside anyone's house apart from Granny's. What was going on?

I didn't like Aunt Mag much. She was a frosty-faced woman who always appeared to be looking down her nose at me. But at least I wouldn't be alone with Uncle Frank, and she wouldn't make me kiss her husband, would she?

The short journey to their house was a blur. All I could think of was what excuse I would give if Uncle Frank asked me to sit on his knee. Perhaps I could say I felt sick or had a headache, or that I had a nasty sore throat or an ulcer on my tongue?

'Come in, Cynthia!' Aunt Mag sang as we got to the front door. 'We've got mutton stew for dinner!'

It smelled foul, but I gave a polite smile. She hadn't drained the fat off the top, and the greasy meat made me want to gag as it slid down my throat.

'Eat up every mouthful, Cynthia,' Aunt Mag warned me sternly.

While I sat there forcing each forkful down my throat, Aunt Mag suddenly vanished from the table. My tummy lurched with fear. I was alone with Uncle Frank, and he had greasy dribble on his chin.

The mutton started to churn in my belly. I realized I really was going to be sick, and I asked if I could go to the toilet, where I immediately vomited up the contents of my stomach.

I hoped now I had finished the dinner I would be able to go home. But where was Aunt Mag?

'Come into the bedroom, you two,' her shrill voice rang out. 'I'm waiting!'

My senses flicked to red alert in an instant. She sounded weird. Why would we go into their bedroom? Frank was ushering me through the bedroom door now, and as I focused on the scene in front of me the blood drained from my face.

Aunt Mag was in the bed. My head swam. The grease on my throat felt like thick slime that was choking me. Then Uncle Frank was in the bed too. They had no clothes on. I could see white flesh. There was naked, flabby skin everywhere. They pulled me into the bed, both laughing.

I saw Uncle Frank's big slimy tongue again. I felt their skin touch my skin, and I saw Aunt Mag touch Uncle Frank, her hands moving quickly over his body.

I cried and retched while they cackled and sniggered. They didn't seem to see my tears at all. They carried on and on until they both seemed to be deliriously happy.

I was crying and trembling when Uncle Frank took me home. Daddy had gone out, so I didn't need to explain where I'd been.

'I hope you behaved yourself,' was all Mammy said as I fell in the door. My eyes were dead. I couldn't speak. 'Thanks for the sherry, Frank!' Mammy called out. 'Same time next week?'

The slam of the door made my head bang and sharpened my numbed senses a little. Surely I wouldn't have to go again?

I sat on the cold lino of the kitchen floor in silence for hours, feeling stunned and sickened. At last I summoned up the energy and courage to speak. There was no way I could face that ordeal again. I had to say something.

'Mammy, I beg you,' I sobbed. 'Please don't make me go back next week. I didn't like it at all! Please don't, Mammy.'

I got no response other than, 'Didn't I tell you to shut up complainin'? Why are you always so awkward?'

I was so afraid I even begged Daddy later, not knowing what sort of trouble that might cause. But to my dismay he didn't seem bothered one bit. 'As long as he doesn't come in this house, I'm not interested!' he bellowed.

So, the following Sunday, I was forced to go though the whole terrifying torture again, only it was worse this time because I knew what to expect, or at least I thought I did.

This time they played games with my mind as well as my body.

I asked for a piece of bread to help me swallow down the lumps of mutton, but Aunt Mag flew into a rage that seemed to come from nowhere. 'You greedy cow – are you saying you're not full?' she yelled. Then she offered me more stew! Was I meant to refuse or accept it? I guessed I should refuse, because she wanted me to be full, but that wasn't right either.

'How dare you turn your nose up, you little bitch.'

After lunch, instead of taking me straight to the bedroom, they said they wanted to show me their collection of dolls. My eyes were watering just looking at them, they were so beautiful. I'd never seen so many in my life. For a few precious seconds, the fear I carried round with me most of the time subsided and I reached out my hand to pick one up.

'Don't you dare touch!' Aunt Mag exclaimed.

Uncle Frank started laughing loudly now, delighting in my shocked expression. 'Don't even think about touching them, you little cow! Bedroom – now!' he ordered.

I started to sob and wail uncontrollably. Through my tears, I could see pretty flowers on the wallpaper and shiny, polished furniture and mirrors lining the walls.

I wondered how anyone who had such a lovely, neat house could be so dirty and wicked. I shut my eyes so I couldn't see their bodies and their creepy smiles, but try as I might I couldn't shut off my other senses.

I didn't want to hear their breathing and panting or their craven laughter. I didn't want to feel their rough, doughy skin against mine. I didn't want to smell Aunt Mag's sickly-sweet perfume or Uncle Frank's stale, sweaty armpits, and I didn't want to taste their pungent breath in my mouth. But I didn't have a choice. I was in bed with them again, and I was their slave.

When I got home that night I felt sick and bruised, and I moved around like a little robot, obeying Mammy's commands and counting the minutes until I could fall asleep and shut down completely. I had hours to wait until Daddy got into bed and hurt me again, and only after that could I relax enough to fall into a fitful sleep.

The next day, after school, Mammy sent me to run up the road because Uncle Frank had something for her.

My heart was in my mouth when I saw him standing there. I had no idea what he might do to me, but to my surprise he smiled broadly and handed me a bottle of sherry and a big white tub for Mammy.

I grabbed them off him quickly, said a polite 'Thank you, Uncle Frank,' and ran home as fast as I could, the contents of the white tub rattling like Smarties in a tube.

I ran down the road past Granny's front door and, to my horror, Aunt Ann was standing on the doorstep with a full mop bucket in her hand.

I was frightened of Aunt Ann. She was a spinster with a twisted face, and she always scowled at me. She shared Granny's house and, when Granny was in, which was most of the time, she just ignored me, but if she saw me on my own she always had a go at me.

A few weeks earlier, she had thrown a bucket of dirty water over me on my way home from school for no reason at all.

If she ever walked past me in the street by chance, she called me a 'little whore' or a 'little bitch' and walloped me with her bag.

Daddy had had fights with Mammy about the way her sister treated me. I'd heard him warn Mammy to get the 'old bitch' to leave me alone. But Mammy always defended 'poor Aunt Ann' and told Daddy I had been cheeky and deserved what she gave me.

I froze when I saw the bucket, but Aunt Ann didn't throw

it. She said, 'See you next week!' in a threatening voice that made my spine tense. What was happening next week?

Mammy explained that Granny was going into hospital, and I was to stay with Aunt Ann to keep her company.

I didn't know what to think. It meant I would be away from Daddy and I could go to sleep without worrying about what he might do to me in bed, and without listening to Mammy and Daddy fighting. I wouldn't wake up itching with that rash on the back of my neck that Daddy seemed to give me. But how would Aunt Ann treat me?

I was very nervous, but I told myself it couldn't be worse than being at home. Aunt Ann was older than Mammy. I didn't think she could do me too much harm. I'd heard all her insults before. If I could avoid getting a soaking from her dirty mop bucket I'd be all right. I'd survive.

I didn't have a choice anyway. 'Off you go, Cynthia! Now look after Aunt Ann, won't you? Don't go giving out any cheek! I'll hear about it if you do!'

My heart sank when I realized I had to share a bed with Aunt Ann. She and Granny shared a bedroom in their tiny terraced house and Aunt Ann said I was to sleep in the same bed as her.

The bed had a mattress that had turned grey and saggy. When I climbed into it, I held my nose. All the bedding absolutely reeked and looked caked with dirt, even worse than our bedding at home.

I felt very tense lying in those filthy bedclothes as I waited for Aunt Ann to come to bed too. I started to fret and panic. Getting into bed with an adult made me feel wary. But Aunt Ann was my old spinster aunt. She wasn't going to touch me, was she? Aunt Mag's face loomed into my mind. Oh God, no! Not Aunt Ann as well! No, I was being silly. I was worrying too much, but I couldn't help it. I was trembling, and my teeth were chattering with cold and fright.

Aunt Ann was in the bed now, wearing a ragged, grey cotton nightdress. My mind hazed over, because I felt something bad was going to happen. It did that a lot lately. My brain just seemed to freeze and close part of itself down. Aunt Ann was leaning over me now, her twisted features far too close to mine. 'You are a dirty little bitch!' she taunted. Her bad breath swamped me, and her teeth looked like they were covered in mould. 'Let's see how much of a dirty little bitch you are!'

She lunged at me and pawed at my chest and legs. Her wrinkled fingertips felt like sandpaper on my skin. I was shocked to the core. I felt like I was bolted to the bed, lying there motionless and powerless against this horrible, smelly woman who seemed to be enjoying making me sob huge tears into the sheets.

I stared at her dressing table while she touched me, desperately trying to take my mind off what was happening. Aunt Ann had perfume bottles, puff powder and sparkly pieces of jewellery. It looked pretty. I wished I was pretty, but I felt very ugly and very dirty. I felt like I would never get rid of her foul fingerprints on my body.

Aunt Ann did the same thing to me many more times over many more months. Telling Mammy would be a waste of time. I knew she would do nothing to help me, but one day I blurted out that I hated Aunt Ann. I just couldn't face going round there again and being subjected to her torture. I told Mammy I hated the way Aunt Ann 'beat' me, but I was too embarrassed to tell her what else she did.

'Why do people treat me like that?' I asked. 'It's not fair, Mammy. Why me?'

'Have you ever thought you must have done something bad to deserve it?' was all Mammy said. Had I?

I tossed her words around in my head for days trying to make sense of them. They really upset me, and made me wonder if I really was as bad as Mammy said. I'd done nothing wrong. I was sure of that. But perhaps I shouldn't be making such a fuss? Was I odd for not liking what Daddy did, and what Mammy had done to me, and now what my uncle and aunts were doing to me? I didn't know. I really wasn't sure. All I knew for certain was that things seemed to be getting worse and worse, and my mind seemed to be feeling foggier and foggier.

Mammy had started sharing her tablets with me when I said I had a sore head. I was very grateful, because my head hurt a lot.

I never got enough sleep, and when I drank the cider Mammy forced on me, it made my head bang even worse instead of helping me fall asleep.

The tablets were the ones Uncle Frank had given her in the big white tub. I saw her crush them up and put them in a sandwich for me once, and in a glass of milk, sometimes when I hadn't even complained about a headache.

The tablets helped, I think. They made my head feel like soft cotton wool. When horrid thoughts came into my head, they seemed to dissolve in the fluff. I couldn't think about them for very long, which was good.

Christmas was coming again. Every time I had a bad night with Daddy or a bad day with Uncle Frank and Aunt Mag, or Aunt Ann, it felt like another bit of my mind clouded over. I wanted to forget all the horrible things, but the way my head felt seemed to spoil the happy things too.

I wasn't really bothered what presents I got, or how we might decorate the house. Granny took us to a party, held by a rich lady. I'd loved it last year, but this time I went through the motions, not really caring if I got the last seat in musical chairs or the last sausage roll. I didn't know why I felt so strange. Maybe I was just growing up? Maybe that was why I didn't giggle and play like the other kids?

I had heard that Mammy was having another baby, but I wasn't excited at first. I was very worried about how we would fit another little one in the house, and how much extra work it would bring me.

One day she asked if I wanted to listen to the baby. I put my ear to her tummy, trying to hear a heartbeat, but I couldn't hear a thing. She allowed me to put my hand on her belly to feel the baby move, and I was amazed when I felt a sharp little kick hit the palm of my hand.

It was incredible, and from that moment on I stopped worrying about how we would manage and started to count down the days until the new baby arrived. It was actually due on Christmas Day. I loved newborn babies, and I couldn't wait to see this one. Christmas suddenly seemed a lot more exciting.

I had no idea how babies were made. I guessed it was one of those things only grown-ups talked about, and I didn't want to make Mammy cross by asking her. It just seemed magical to me.

The big day was drawing very close now. Food and drink were arriving at the house daily, and Daddy won a giant turkey in a pub raffle, which he seemed to do every year.

I had the usual tussle with Daddy about getting him to hand over his money for my present, but I didn't let it spoil things. Whatever nightmares happened to me in bed were pushed out of my head as far as possible too. Why should those horrible things spoil Christmas? I didn't have to think about them all the time, did I?

Mammy was very big, her bulging tummy pushing up the front of her dresses so the hem curved up, making the skirt look a foot shorter at the front than the back. She'd bought a new black pram for the baby too, and I couldn't wait for it to arrive.

I was disappointed when I woke up on Christmas morning, because the baby was still in Mammy's tummy. Mammy had got all the dinner prepared the day before again, and she looked tired, and Daddy just stayed in bed.

When Mammy told me to take Daddy his dinner up, I thought I would faint. I instantly and vividly remembered what had happened the Christmas before, but I didn't cry.

I pushed my feelings deep inside me, squashing and hiding them deep down. I walked up the stairs with the dinner like an obedient servant, my head all thick and heavy with dread.

There was a lightbulb in the bedroom, as a special treat for Christmas. I switched the light on, but Daddy boomed, 'Switch it off – and come here!'

I hesitated, and the plate started to wobble in my hands.

'Get here now, you!' he growled. I put the plate down on the dressing table and got onto the bed.

His hands were on me now, pulling off my underwear while I flopped about like the yellow-haired rag dolly Mary was playing with downstairs. His eyes looked dead and his mouth was set in a snarl. Usually, it was very dark when he did these things, and even though I had switched off the light as instructed, the fact it was daylight outside and there was some light trickling through the side of the blanket on the window meant I could see Daddy clearly. It made everything seem more real and more menacing.

Now he was behind me, thank God. I didn't have to look

at his face as I lay frozen solid while he did what he wanted to do.

My bottom hurt, and I stared at the Christmas dinner going cold on the plate, trying to take my mind off the pain.

It felt more intense than ever and seemed to set my whole spine on fire. The food looked disgusting as the gravy glazed over it. I let my eyes glaze over too. I wanted to be in a foggy bubble. I wanted to be anywhere but here.

In the end, baby Michael didn't arrive until 12 January 1971. He was an incredibly pretty baby, and my mammy proudly put him in the big black pram she'd bought for him. I was delighted to have a new baby brother and willingly threw myself into helping out with bottle feeds and changing nappies.

Not long afterwards, I found out my big sister Margaret was having a baby too. Margaret was seventeen, and seemed very grown-up and sophisticated to me. She had her baby girl in hospital in August that same year.

Daddy caused a huge row that night. He shouted at Mammy and told her Margaret had to have the baby adopted, which I think meant the baby had to live with somebody else. I cried in bed when I heard him say that. The baby was called Theresa, and I was longing to see her.

'We're not having another baby in this house – no way!' Daddy bellowed. 'There are already too many of us here. Michael is only seven months old!'

Mammy argued and wailed and pleaded with Daddy for

three days and nights after she had been to visit Margaret and Theresa in hospital.

'You've got to let the baby come home,' she begged. 'I'm not allowing that child to be adopted. Think of poor Margaret! Think of the child!'

The more Daddy argued, the more Mammy dug her heels in, until eventually she ran away for three days in protest.

The house felt calmer without her, and I didn't miss her at all. It was a relief not to have her around, but I wanted Mammy to come back so she could keep fighting to have the baby brought home. It didn't seem fair that baby Theresa couldn't live with us.

Daddy sent me and Peter out to search for Mammy in the end, and we walked for miles before finding her, sitting down on the pier in Dun Laoghaire, smoking a cigarette.

'Tell your father I'm not coming home until he lets poor baby Theresa home,' she shouted. 'Go on, tell him.'

Peter and I ran home anxiously with the news, knowing it would infuriate Daddy, but knowing we had to risk his temper, otherwise Mammy, Margaret and the baby might never come home.

'This has gone on long enough!' he roared. 'I don't want any more shame brought on this family. Tell your Mammy to come home – and the baby can come too!'

I will never forget the first time I saw Theresa. Margaret carried her home from hospital in a pink blanket, and I had to stand on the dwarf wall in the front garden to peep inside the bundle. My heart melted, and I fell in love with her instantly.

She was perfect, and I wished her arrival would bring good things. By now, I knew better than to get my hopes up, though. From the moment I saw her, I was afraid that her being there would cause more rows and trouble at home.

Chapter 11

Daddy's Friends

'Come on, Cynthia, we're goin' out!' Mammy said, pulling me out of bed.

It was very dark in the bedroom. Black blobs danced around in my head. I must have been fast asleep, because I hadn't heard Mammy come in. 'Get dressed quick!' she hissed.

'Why, Mammy, what's happening?' I stuttered. I felt scared, yet I was still half asleep. I didn't know where I was. Why was Mammy pulling me out of bed?

'Your da is already up there!' The black shapes stopped me from thinking properly. I wanted to wake up fully. I wanted to snap out of my sleep, but I couldn't. My head felt fuzzy. My brain felt like a heavy iron ball slamming around, banging on my skull. The pavement was wet and the air felt damp. My legs were freezing and my eyeballs felt icy cold in my woolly head. Mammy was taking me somewhere. 'Keep walking! Act normal!' she said.

Mammy knew where she was going. 'Daddy is already up there,' she said again, breathlessly. It felt as if I was going through a dark tunnel. I didn't argue, I just kept walking, feeling like I was sleepwalking through the streets.

'We're here! Here we are, Cynthia!' Mammy said at last. I looked up and saw a creepy-looking building.

I'd never been here before. Why was I here now? Why did Daddy want me here with him in the middle of the night?'

I turned round to ask Mammy what was happening, but she had gone. She had pushed me in the door, and I was standing in a big, cold room on my own.

There were more dark shapes now, but they weren't in my head. They were in front of my eyes. The shapes started moving and talking. 'She's pretty!' one of the shapes said. 'Who's first then?'

Candles flickered, and I could see faces lighting up inside the black shapes. I recognized Daddy's face, and there were lots of other men too; I could hear them laughing as they came towards me.

My whole head felt like a bulging black cloud now. I wanted it to explode. I wanted to cry and shout, but my body wasn't working properly. When the men started touching me and passing me around, I felt like I was wading through concrete that was slowly setting around my limbs.

I couldn't control my body at all. They seemed to be able to move me around however they wanted.

They lay me on a table and took turns to hurt me really badly while the others watched. They were smiling and enjoying themselves, but I was in agony. Couldn't they see? I think I passed out.

Mammy was waiting outside afterwards, and she gave me the biggest smile I had ever seen on her face when she pulled me back out the door. 'Let's go, Cynthia!' she said, linking her arm through mine and taking my weight. She practically carried me home, and threw me back in bed like a sack of dirty laundry.

I blacked out the second my head hit the pillow. When I woke up I thought I'd had a nightmare. I could see the candles, the sweaty legs and ugly skin, and I could hear the men's menacing laughter. I touched my face and legs and arms in disbelief. I remembered the night before, the horror. And I'd missed school. I'd woken up far too late, and nobody had bothered to get me up.

Mammy was still sleeping, so I crept out of the back door and ran to the building, retracing my steps in floods of tears. I sat on the curb outside for hours, until my whole body felt numb. It was as if I was only half there. I stared at every window, wondering if I might see one of the men again. Had it really happened? I knew it had, but I didn't want to believe it. I wished it was a nightmare. Why was my mind so foggy? My head was pounding. What on earth had gone on? All the black shapes danced around in my head like ghosts, haunting and taunting me.

Someone I recognized rode past on a bike and shouted, 'Hi, Cynthia! How you doin'?' That cheery voice snapped me out of my trance, and I suddenly thought, Oh God, Daddy will kill me if he sees me here! I ran straight home, feeling sick with confusion.

It must have been Tuesday now, because when I got home Mammy sent me to the post office for our Children's Allowance money. It always got paid on the first Tuesday of the month, and it was always my job to collect it then go to the shops.

She said nothing about the night before. I was relieved she seemed to be acting normal and wasn't cross with me for running out without telling her, but then she said that this month, she had some special instructions for me. She explained that once I'd collected the allowance money, I was to put it away in my pocket and not spend it on shopping like I normally did.

I was confused, because she then went on to tell me what food and drink we needed, and where to fetch it from. She gave me specific addresses I had to visit to collect the shopping, but emphasized that I didn't need to pay for any of it.

It sounded crazy, but I nodded. It seemed that if I went to the places she told me to and said certain things, phrases Mammy taught me, I'd be given the goods we wanted.

It all seemed very weird, but I didn't bother arguing. I felt exhausted, and I just nodded and repeated what she told me, as if I was a puppet.

I was glad to get back out of the house. I was concentrating hard, because my head hurt. At the first address, I knocked nervously on the door, not convinced that Mammy's plan would work. It seemed so odd. The man who answered went all red in the face and twitchy when he saw me. He ushered his wife out the back and, to my amazement, without me saying a word, he gave me a bag of things before shooing me away and slamming his door shut in a hurry. At the second place, the man scowled at me and told me to 'get lost' as he thrust a bottle of sherry at me.

A few of the men just looked startled, but they kept their cool. 'My mammy sent me, she wants to know have you anything going spare?' I asked. 'My mammy said have you anything you're throwing out?' They all handed me things, and not one of them asked for any money.

I died with shame on one street, because some of my class-mates were passing in their neat clothes and with fancy ribbons in their hair, but I still said my lines. Going home empty-handed was not an option. I was afraid Mammy would explode and hit me, so I had to keep coming out with these embarrassing phrases.

Sometimes all I had to say was: 'My granny sent me, she wants to know do you have anything for her...' I wouldn't even finish my sentence before the men scuttled off to fetch me a bag and send me on my way.

I ended up laden down with food and drink, and some-times I was also given a thick brown envelope to hand to Mammy or Granny.

I was ordered to go through the strange ritual every day after I had been taken to the scary building.

Eventually, as I stood in front of the men, month after month, watching them squirm, I had to accept that what happened in the scary place was definitely no nightmare. It was very real, because these were the same men who terrified and hurt me in that creepy old building.

Sometimes when I was taken there, I was so drowsy I could barely remember a thing afterwards. Phrases rang in my ears for ages, and I was reminded of them when I least expected it, like when I was sitting in a class or helping change the babies:

'She's my favourite! I like her, she's the best.' I was always sore and thick-headed for many days afterwards, but the words pierced through the fog, making me tremble and worry. I remembered these words when I faced the men the next day, but they barely spoke to me when I was asking them for my 'shopping'. It was their turn to be horrified as they thrust out their sweaty hands and sent me on my way with Mammy's requests.

One night, Mammy came into the creepy building with me. She touched me like some of the men did. I felt so sick, and everything went black. Some time later, I saw she had the biggest bundle of cash in her hand I had ever seen. I was scared to walk beside her when we went home, but I had no choice. 'Hurry up, Cynthia!' she scolded. 'Get a move on!' My legs felt like lead, and I felt as if I was floating all the way home, with Mammy's snarling voice pushing me along, warning me not to stop and to just 'act normal'.

When I gave Granny the brown envelope the next day,

she said, 'Thanks, Cynthia, love,' and gave me a sweet smile. She took some of the notes out and put them in another envelope, then told me to walk the few miles to Killiney to donate money to the nuns who looked after the African babies.

I thought how kind she was. I knew babies were starving in Africa, because Mother Felicity had told me often enough, pointing at half-eaten sandwiches at school. I knew Granny didn't have much money, so I thought she was a great lady to make a donation to the black babies.

Around this time, I had my first period.

I was sitting up in bed one Saturday morning and had pulled back the black blanket from the window to let in a shard of light, as I wanted to cut up some paper.

Mammy didn't allow me to play with scissors, so I'd smuggled a pair upstairs and hidden them under the bedclothes.

Suddenly I felt as if I'd wet myself. I peered tentatively under the blankets, and gasped when I saw fresh blood.

I was very frightened because I thought I'd cut myself badly with the scissors, so I confessed to Mammy what I'd done and she ordered me downstairs to the kitchen sink to wash myself.

I tore up an old rag and mopped up as much blood as I could, but it wouldn't stop flowing. Now it was dripping down my leg, and I was starting to panic. Where was it coming from?

'Mammy!' I screamed. 'I can't stop the blood! Please help me!'

'You must have got your "things",' she said in a disinterested voice. 'Go into your sisters' drawer and get those things they wear and put one in your knickers.'

I had seen the white towels in my sisters' room before. I knew that they were some kind of pad you put in your knickers, but my mammy didn't explain anything to me and I had no idea why I was having 'things' or what they were.

I stuffed the pad in my knickers and asked Mammy what I should do next.

She told me I couldn't take my sisters' things again, because they paid for them with the money they earned in their factory jobs.

'Tear up some old rags and put them in your knickers,' Mammy told me, and never said another word on the matter ever again.

I was only ten-years-old, and every month I felt frightened and upset when I started to bleed, because I had no idea when my 'things' would come or how long they would last.

I went rummaging under the stairs for old towels and jumpers to cut up, and I walked around feeling dirtier than ever. Though Mammy never talked about my 'things', she seemed to know when I was having them, and every time I was bleeding, she woke me up in my bed at night quite unexpectedly.

The first time it happened, I thought she was taking me to the building, because that was usually the reason she woke me up at night. I immediately started trembling and gasping for air in a panic, but Mammy didn't drag me out of bed. She raked at my face with her fingernails and bellowed, 'You're a whore! You're a prostitute! You're a dirty bitch.'

I did feel dirty, but I didn't know what a whore or a prostitute was. I knew they were bad words, but I didn't know why *I* was so bad. Mammy did the same thing every time I was bleeding, and it just became part of my routine. 'Things' to me meant panicking at the sight of the blood, tearing up old rags and feeling more filthy and uncomfortable than ever, and expecting Mammy to wake me in the night to claw at my face with her fingernails and insult me.

The blood didn't seem to bother Daddy or anybody else, as the men still touched me down below and carried on hurting me. But it seemed to send Mammy mad.

Maybe she didn't want me to be a big girl like my sisters. I couldn't understand her, but I could tell I was growing up.

One day ran into the next. Nothing excited me or surprised me any more. Every day was like a survival exercise. I had to get through it, and then I had to get through the night.

Some days I felt very groggy, too groggy. Mammy was giving me lots of tablets now, and I was even starting to get scared of the food she gave me, in case it was my sandwiches that were making me so groggy I couldn't remember anything at all. I tried to make my own food, or throw the sandwiches away when Mammy wasn't looking.

I wondered why I couldn't be like everyone else. I wanted to grow up faster. I didn't like being a little girl. The only time I liked it was when I spent time with Granny. I still loved to sit by her legs and listen to her ghost stories.

Sometimes I pretended I was sick just so I could have the day off school and go round to her house, or I would play truant if Mammy wouldn't let me stay off. Aunt Ann worked during the day, so it was the perfect opportunity to spend uninterrupted time with my lovely, kind Granny.

She told me terrifying stories about the devil sometimes. I sat wide-eyed and open-mouthed with fright as she told me how the devil haunted St Patrick's Road, which ran alongside her street.

'A priest used to walk up and down St Patrick's Road at midnight saying prayers to rid the devil from the roofs of the houses,' she told me. 'But the priest mysteriously died on the road one night, and now his ghost walks up and down St Patrick's Road! If you're really lucky, Cynthia, you might see the devil and the ghost of the priest!'

I lapped up her stories hungrily, even though they scared me, because at least they let me escape the horrors of my own life for a while.

Chapter 12

Mammy's Friend

Something snapped in me one night.

I was feeling more angry than terrified when I went to bed. The night before, I had got so sick of what Daddy did to me I had gone downstairs when he finished and told Mammy plainly I didn't like what Daddy was doing to me 'down there'. The pain had got so bad I just couldn't take it any more.

I pushed aside the scary memories I had about what Mammy did to me when she changed the beds, and what she did to me in the building. Whatever she did, she was still my mammy, wasn't she? So maybe she might just help me after all.

'Mammy, I have something to tell you. I don't like what Daddy is doing to me "down there",' I said. I had rehearsed what I was going to say about twenty times in my head. I was too embarrassed to talk about 'private parts' and, anyway, Mammy was always saying they were filthy bits of my body. But I was sure she would know what I was talking about this time.

She hesitated for a moment, as if thinking about what to say. I willed her to tell me she would stop Daddy hurting me, that she would make sure Daddy never touched me again.

'Oh, Cynthia!' she said finally. She had a half-smile on her lips, but her eyes were dead. 'He's just rollin' over drunk in his sleep. Haven't I already told you that before?'

'Yes – but that was when I told you I didn't like what he did in bed,' I stammered. 'What I really mean is I don't like what he does to me...down below.'

'Rollin' over drunk,' she repeated casually. 'Stop complaining. You're makin' trouble.' My heart went thump. That was the end of the conversation, because Mammy immediately shooed me back up to bed, where I lay fretting and crying, feeling trapped and totally alone.

Now it was the next evening, and I was in the back bedroom, sensing I faced another long night of putting up with pain. I felt very drowsy and tired and fell into a patchy, fear-filled sleep.

Suddenly, I saw a man looming over my bed, I didn't even realize he was there until it was too late. I snapped open my eyes in terror, smelling danger, and was shocked to see it was a 'friend' of Mammy's I called the thug.

Mammy knew I was particularly scared of this thug, but she had clearly given him free rein to come into my bedroom and do what he liked to me while my daddy was out drinking. I was exhausted mentally as well as physically, but I made an instinctive decision that night.

I sat up tall and looked him straight in the eye.

'No way!' I screamed. 'I just can't take any more.' I had reached absolute breaking point and this man wanting to hurt me was the final straw.

I thought I might be able to fight him off. I was quite small and skinny, and he was much stronger and bigger than me, but I lashed out with all my might.

His eyes flashed angrily. My bold talk seemed to enrage him and make him more aggressive. 'Oh yeah? Try and fuckin' stop me,' he snarled.

He made a grab for me, and I struggled, kicking and lashing out with my fists for all I was worth. I felt tiny and helpless, but I wasn't giving up. I really couldn't take any more.

Suddenly I was aware he was hovering high above me. He was standing on the pillows, holding on to the big wooden headboard behind me.

I screwed my eyes shut in a blind panic, realizing what he was about to do. *Stamp!* went his heavy foot, down on to my face.

I felt something snap, and the pain was excruciating. *Stamp!* he went again, cursing and shouting at me as he lifted his foot ready for the next blow.

I felt blood coming from my nose as he stamped on my face again and again. As I lay there writhing in pain, he had his way with me.

I went to Mammy afterwards, once I eventually found the

strength to lift myself off the bed and stagger downstairs. 'That thug stamped on my face!'

She was sitting by the fire drinking her favourite sherry, and she didn't look up. 'Stop being such a complainin' little bitch.'

I begged her to take me to the doctor's, but she refused and sent me back to bed. I'd heard her say before that Daddy's wage was too high for us to get free medical care. I guessed that was why she never took me to the doctor.

The thug visited me in bed many more times. I never had any warning, and he had a habit of appearing from nowhere.

I often went to school with black eyes and bruises. I'd get fresh bruises on top of old ones, so my skin was always pitted with varying shades of black, blue and yellow marks. When I looked particularly bad, I just tried to make myself invisible at the back of the class and keep out of everyone's way. Nobody at school seemed to notice, or perhaps they just thought I got into lots of fights.

Mammy said nothing. She seemed quite happy to sit downstairs drinking and smoking and turning a blind eye to what happened to me upstairs night after night. I felt so weak and exhausted, like my body was being broken over and over again. I wanted to fight, but I felt like a tiny speck compared to my abusers. There had to be another way of escaping them.

As summer turned to winter, I started pretending I wanted to use the toilet to get out of the bedroom and away from the possibility of more pain and terror.

I figured that the thug couldn't get me if I was in the outside toilet in the back garden. It was dark and damp and stank so badly it made my eyes well up and sting, but it was better than lying terrified in bed.

Sometimes I huddled out there for ages, imagining spiders crawling over me, but it was far better than lying in bed and waiting for the thug to crawl on top of me, knowing Mammy was downstairs pretending nothing was happening. Or maybe she hated me so much she was even enjoying the fact I was suffering so badly?

One night, I was standing in the toilet in my vest and knickers. It was a bitterly cold night, and I was wondering how long I could stand it before I would be forced to go back inside.

All of a sudden, my nerves started to twang, and I felt myself physically shaking with cold and fear.

I could hear a strange noise outside, above my head. Someone was prowling around. I listened so intently that I could hear my own blood pumping through my veins. It was him looking for me, I just knew it. He didn't come in that time, but he made it clear he had worked out what I was up to. I knew it was only a matter of time before my plan stopped working.

That time arrived just a few nights later, when he hid in the toilet, behind the door, waiting for me. When I crept in, hoping for a few minutes' peace, he slammed the door shut, put his hand over my mouth and hurt me very quickly, and very violently. Afterwards he shared a laugh and a joke with my mammy.

There was no escape. I felt utterly trapped. I wasn't strong enough to fight him off, and it felt like the only weapon I had was my mind.

I tried to switch it off whenever he appeared. I didn't want to feel anything or think anything. If I emptied my brain and let it fuzz over, I would feel less hurt and pain. It worked a bit, but not as much as I would have liked.

It was impossible to feel normal. Daddy was still hurting me too. Sometimes, when the thug had finished with me for the night, he would go and Mammy would send me to sleep in the front bedroom again, and Daddy would roll in from the pub and attack me too. I rarely got through a night without one or both of them forcing themselves on me.

Other girls at school chatted about what they had done at the weekend or watched on TV. They had family gatherings, walks to church and shopping trips with their mammies. I didn't do any of those things, and I felt left out.

I just couldn't talk to my friends, in case I really was a very bad person. What would they think of me?

They wouldn't want to hear about the time in the building when the men put me in a different room, then all queued up outside the door and took it in turns to come in and hurt me. In fact, no one would want to know any of what happened to me. Having all those men there simply to do terrible things to me was too traumatic to contemplate. Who would want to hear about all that? It was sickening.

Sometimes the men sat on chairs in a row and passed me

round while they all laughed loudly. I didn't want to even think about it myself, let alone tell my friends.

At least when I was in school I knew nobody was going to hurt me in the way Daddy and the other men did.

I loved fooling around with my friends. Even though the posh kids kept out of my way or looked down on me for my scruffy appearance, I didn't care. I had my own mates, and when I was making them roar with laughter with my impression of Mother Dorothy, nose pointed in the air and pretend cane swishing in my hand, I felt great. 'You are all SINNERS!' I'd hiss theatrically. We'd all fall about in hysterics, and it felt so good to switch off from my worries and be myself for a little while.

I relished those golden moments, too, when I could read quietly and enjoy the peace, and on days when my head felt clear I really enjoyed learning. Mother Dorothy still gave out steam to me the whole time, and I never knew when my peace or fun might be snatched away and I'd be punished and shamed, but still, I much preferred being at school to being at home. Home meant horror. Home meant scary, violent thugs forcing themselves on me in the dark and hurting me. Home meant never knowing what Daddy might do. Home meant Mammy drinking and smoking and telling me I was a complaining bitch, I was crazy, I was a devil child; It was all my fault. I hated being at home.

Still, though, the one place I always felt better was by Granny's side. I felt protected and safe, but I couldn't tell Granny about all the strange and frightening things in my life, could I? I didn't want to spoil my special time with her, it was too precious to ruin. I'd be beaten so badly by Mammy and Daddy that life wouldn't be worth living. No, I couldn't tell Granny.

I started visiting Granny more than ever. I went most lunchtimes and played truant from school whenever I could just so I could enjoy a bit of peace and friendly company. Sipping hot, sweet tea in her living room was a real tonic. It instantly pepped me up and made me feel a bit happier inside.

I felt the knots in my shoulders loosen when I walked to Granny's. I could feel them easing with every step I took down the road and round the corner.

I would wonder if Granny might have some fruit for me, or maybe some broken biscuits. She always had a treat of some kind in store. Being with Granny felt so special. Hers was the only house I ever really visited, apart from Uncle Frank's. She made me feel welcome and loved and safe.

I never got invited into any of my friends' houses. They sometimes said they were sorry not to be able to invite me, but their mammies wouldn't let them. I knew they were telling the truth, because I sometimes knocked on their door and their mammies told me flatly, 'No, you can't come in,' or 'No, she can't play with you.'

I guessed it was because I always looked so dirty and messy, not a little girl anyone would want their child playing with. Anyhow, I could visit Granny whenever I wanted, and I loved my Granny.

'Come in, Cynthia!' would beam kindly when I knocked on the door at lunchtime.

'Sit yourself down by the fire while I fetch you a cup of tea. I've got wafers today, lovely pink ones.'

I would smile back at Granny and settle myself on the floor. 'Can you show me the Irish jig?' I might ask. She was quite an old lady – she must have been about seventy-years-old – but she often got up and showed me the jig. 'Please, Granny?'

'Maybe later,' she'd say, smiling. 'Drink up your tea for now.'

A smile from Granny made me feel special. I loved visiting her. Mammy made me go there to do her cleaning and shopping, but I didn't mind at all, I preferred being there than being at home.

Since the two new babies had arrived, things had got even tougher for me there.

Mammy expected me to look after all four of my younger siblings, and I found it really hard trying to help them all get dressed and give them their breakfast before school.

I was coming up to eleven now. Mary was seven, Martin was five, Michael was about eighteen months, and Theresa was a year old. Every morning I fed all four kids with Weetabix with sugar on, wiped their faces, kissed the babies goodbye and took Mary and Martin to school with me.

I always held their hands, like the mammies did, because I remembered how much I liked it when Esther used to hold my hand on the way to school.

Our mammy just stayed in bed.

I worried about the babies when I was out. I always left them in clean nappies, even if it meant tearing up old sheets and towels and wrapping them round their wriggling bottoms.

But they were always dirty and smelly when I got home at lunchtime to give them a slice of bread or some mashed-up potato and corned beef. Their little feet would be blue with cold too. I felt sorry for them.

Theresa was a very sweet, calm baby who never made much fuss and greeted me with great big smiles, but Michael hardly ever seemed happy.

Often when I came in, he would be rocking back and forth in a chair, or banging his head off a wall and crying. It made me really sad to see him like that, and I gave him extra cuddles.

After school, I went to the local shops for cigarettes and more bread or meat and vegetables. From time to time Mammy sent me to Dun Laoghaire with an old pram to fetch coal. It was three miles away, and my legs ached, but Mammy always warned me not to argue, and I didn't want the babies to be cold so I always fetched the coal.

Sometimes we needed briquettes for the fire too. They had wire carriers around them that cut my hands, but I didn't bother complaining. Most of the time I carried bags of turf and sacks of potatoes on my back. I got so tired in the evening my arms and legs felt as if lead weights, but I'd always help make the dinner. It felt as if I'd peeled a million spuds, but Mammy usually did the actual cooking.

If she was in a good mood, she made nice things, like burgers or chops with cabbage and turnips, but if she was in a bad mood or was very tired, we dipped bread into a dissolved Oxo cube or spread it with tomato ketchup.

By 7 p.m. I'd be dropping with tiredness, but I had to walk back to the shops to buy more cigarettes and alcohol for Mammy.

One day I asked her if I could buy all the shopping in one go, instead of making three separate trips. The local shops were only a ten-minute walk away, but I got fed up with all the walking and going in the same shops over and over again.

'No way!' was all Mammy said.

'But I'm tired, Mammy. I could get everything we need at lunchtime! Why do I have to go at four o'clock and seven o'clock? I'm really tired.'

'No way!' she repeated angrily. 'Are you arguing with me?' Her fist was raised, and I knew that if I said yes she would punch me.

'No, Mammy, I am not arguing,' I said.

'Good. Don't be such lazy bitch. Just do it.'

When I climbed into bed, I'd be desperate for sleep, but my chores for the day were still not over. The thug was still attacking me in bed whenever he felt like it. Mammy seemed to have given him an open invitation into my bedroom whenever Daddy was still in the pub.

Daddy was still regularly hurting me in bed in the early

hours of the morning, once he'd staggered home, usually the worse for drink, and once a month I was still being dragged to that horrible building with all those scary men.

When I had my 'thing' and I bled every month, I felt more tired still, but still none of the men left me alone. The blood made me feel messy and dirty, but none of the people who touched my body seemed to be bothered by it.

I felt ashamed of the old rags and cut-up jumpers in my knickers.

Uncle Frank and Aunt Mag called me a dirty bitch whether I was bleeding or not, and so did Aunt Ann, though they were touching me less and less these days.

Some of the men in the building remarked on it, and even seemed to like seeing my blood. I could never forget the leering comments they made, even though, every time I went there, I felt like bits of my brain had fallen out of my head.

Daddy never spoke to me in bed, apart from to tell me sometimes it was 'Mammy's fault' he was hurting me. 'Get here now, you!' he said most nights, and after that he just grunted.

I wondered if my life would ever change. I thought about my big sister Esther and wondered if maybe one day I could get on a boat and sail away like she did.

Margaret had sailed away now too. I heard Mammy and Daddy discussing how she had gone off to start a new job. Theresa wasn't two yet, and it was decided that Mammy and Daddy would adopt her.

I was about to join fifth class at school. I was nearly eleven, and I looked forward to being one of the bigger girls in the school. I was growing up fast.

I hoped that maybe now I was a big girl my life might finally change for the better. It couldn't get worse, could it?

Chapter 13

'You're Having a Baby'

I loved joining fifth class, and I was delighted to meet our teacher. She was young and pretty with blond hair.

She looked so much kinder than Mother Dorothy, and I noticed from the very first day that I got asked the same questions and was given the same chances to join in as all the posh kids.

If I didn't have a pencil or a copy book the teacher always managed to find me one, and when I told her I 'forgot' my cookery ingredients she gave me a kind look, like she understood and had actually been there when Daddy said, 'No way! I'm not givin' you the money. Your mother can teach you to cook!'

Our teacher gave us singing lessons, and I loved joining in with the songs she taught us, like 'Lord of the Dance' and 'Morning Has Broken'. All my friends told me I had a great voice, and when I belted out those songs I felt like a singer on a stage. At break time I sang 'Brown Sugar' by the Rolling Stones and put on pretend shows for my friends, holding an invisible microphone and kicking my legs.

Every morning when I opened my eyes, I really looked forward to school. It wasn't just because I could have a laugh with my friends and enjoyed escaping from home, I was learning new things every day, and I found out I was good at reading and writing, and could even do maths better than I ever had before.

Now I was bigger, I washed myself with a bucket of water and a rag and managed to clean my clothes sometimes, too, after Esther visited and brought us soap and washing powder.

Nobody called me smelly any more, and even though my head still itched, I felt better about my appearance. The horrible things that happened outside of school still happened but, for the first time, they didn't feel like they were the whole of my life.

Daddy had bought us a black Yorkshire terrier, and we named him Charlie. I loved him to bits. He would follow me to school every day and wait for me outside the school gates until I came out at lunchtime. He was very special, and I loved him dearly. He made me smile.

I hadn't been in my new class very long when I started to feel sick a lot. It wasn't much after my eleventh birthday.

It was a very strange sort of sickness. It wasn't like the way I felt sick when Aunt Mag made me eat her disgusting mutton stew, or when Mammy mashed up those pills from the big white tub into my sandwiches, which I now knew said 'Valium' on the side.

This sickness was different from any other sickness I'd felt before. I had this funny feeling in my stomach all the time and I felt sort of dizzy. The strange thing about it was that I didn't feel I was actually going to be sick, it was just a constant feeling of having a queasy tummy.

It went on for days and days, and eventually weeks. At first I was scared of telling Mammy about it because I didn't want any more of that medicine in case it made me feel worse. I'd worked out that the white pills gave me sickening headaches and made me dizzy and forgetful, so I didn't want any of those. I'd prefer just to feel sick.

The sickness just wouldn't go away though, and in the end I decided I had better tell someone. I didn't want to tell the nuns because I didn't want to be sent home from school, so one night I told Mammy.

'Mammy, I feel sick and want to vomit, but nothing's coming out,' I explained. 'What's wrong with me?'

I was relieved that Mammy didn't ignore me. In fact, she seemed to know what to do straight away. She didn't shout at me for complaining, and she didn't try to give me those white pills either, so I was very glad I had told her my problem.

'Drink a pint of salt and water,' she told me firmly.

She didn't seem worried, and didn't even get out of her rocking chair or put down her tumbler of port. It couldn't be anything serious. 'Just go and drink a pint of salt and water, Cynthia,' she said with confidence.

I felt relieved I was getting a cure, even though I retched as I forced the disgusting salt water down my throat.

I was very disappointed when I didn't vomit or feel any better, but thankfully Mammy knew what to do. 'Add more salt,' she told me. 'Add as much as you can.' I poured in huge spoonfuls, but Mammy's cure still didn't work. I wasn't sick, I just had a raging thirst.

When I went to bed, I prayed that I'd wake up feeling better the next day, but I didn't. As soon as I opened my eyes the sickness swept over me. I felt worse instead of better, but I'd noticed the mornings were always worse.

My tummy felt weird now too. I didn't feel like eating my Weetabix for breakfast, and when I got the little ones ready for school my head was spinning.

Changing the babies' nappies made me gag, but still I couldn't be sick. I just felt nauseous, it was so weird. I didn't want to tell Mammy again in case she made me drink more salt water. It hadn't helped, and it tasted foul. I didn't want any more of that.

So I put up with the sick feeling for what felt like weeks, hoping every day it would just go away.

One day, I was sitting at my desk concentrating hard on a maths problem on the board, when I felt something fly inside my stomach.

It felt exactly like a butterfly, but not like the type of

butterflies I got when I felt scared. This felt like I really had a butterfly fluttering its wings inside me.

I didn't know what to do, so I just sat there feeling strange. I didn't mention it to anyone, not even my friends at school. I thought they would think I was weird or telling one of my silly stories to entertain them. Maybe I was imagining it? No, I felt it again and again. I held my book low down across my tummy in case you could actually see my tummy move.

The sickness was still there too, and now I had something fluttering inside me. What if I had something seriously wrong with me? I had to talk to Mammy again. Hopefully, this time, she would know of a better cure.

'Have a pint of salt water,' Mammy told me again sternly. 'Put as much salt in as you can.' I groaned at the thought of that salt water, but I thought Mammy must know best.

She didn't seem worried about the fluttering when I told her about it. She didn't frown or do anything but sit in her chair drinking. Perhaps I was making a fuss about nothing?

'Go and buy some vitamin tablets,' she said in the end, after I'd made a scene of drinking down some salt water with the tiniest bit of salt I could get away with. It made me retch, but nothing came up.

Mammy sent me to the shop and told me exactly which vitamins to buy. They were called Haliborange, and she announced later that all the children in the house were to take them.

'Line up now,' she ordered the younger kids. I felt pleased

that Mammy was trying to help me get over my sickness. She was looking after me, and she was making sure the little ones didn't get sick too. She'd never given us vitamins before, and they weren't cheap either. I'd been surprised how much money she gave me to go to the shop.

Mammy dished out a tablet to each child in turn, but when she got to me at the end of the line she put the box of Haliborange down and brought out a dark bottle of medicine, telling me that, because I was older, I needed different vitamins.

It was dark, thick, sticky liquid that looked like treacle but tasted a bit fishy. It was foul, but I dutifully licked the spoon clean, hoping my sickness and funny tummy would get better soon.

Mammy told me to keep taking the salt water too, just to 'make sure', and so I did, but all that happened was that I started to feel even more unwell.

I couldn't understand it. I was drinking pints of salt water, eating raw eggs and liver and taking my vitamin mixture, all of which were meant to 'do me good', so why weren't they helping?

I didn't look ill. We all had Mammy's fine skin, and I had roses in my cheeks. I was still feeling very sick in the mornings, though, and in the afternoons I was exhausted.

When I complained to Mammy that I didn't seem to be getting better, she just told me to keep drinking the salt water and taking the vitamins. In the end I stopped complaining.

Daddy didn't seem worried at all. One night I felt so weary

and my head ached so much I begged him to leave me alone. 'Daddy, please, no,' I said. 'I think I'll be sick.'

'Get here now!' he sneered, tying his belt around my chest. 'You know what happens if you start!' As he tightened the buckle, I could feel my heart beating ferociously in my chest. It was going so fast I was sure it would burst out and snap that leather belt right off me.

I wished I actually could be sick, thinking that would make Daddy get off me. My stomach was doing somersaults. He smelled worse than usual tonight. He'd used the toilet bucket, and the room smelled overpoweringly vile too. I wished I could vomit all over him, but I just lay there feeling sick and helpless and suffocated by his sweat and reeking breath.

The next day, I was sitting behind my desk listening to the teacher when I felt something move sharply inside me. It felt like a kick. It wasn't a flutter like before. It was unmistakably a kick. But how could something kick me inside my stomach? What had got in there?

I stared at the blackboard and tried to work it out. What could the explanation be? What illness could make something feel like it was kicking me inside the tummy?

I looked around at my classmates. They were all just staring at the blackboard or looking bored and jotting notes like always. Everything looked so normal, but I felt detached, like I was on a different planet from everybody else. I looked round again and felt a wave of loneliness sweep over me. I knew I couldn't tell anyone what had just happened. How could I? I didn't even know what it was, so how could I explain it? People might laugh at me or think I was mad.

I had to talk to Mammy again. She had helped the first time, rushing me out to buy vitamins, so she must care about this and she would help me again.

I raced up to her bedside as soon as I got in from school.

'Mammy, something's banging inside my stomach,' I told her. 'It's scaring me.'

I looked at Mammy intently, desperately hoping she would have another answer, or another medicine that might work better. She looked back at me with no expression in her eyes. 'You're having a baby,' she said in a harsh, frosty voice.

The room around me started to shift. The walls wobbled and the floor tilted. Nothing was still except for Mammy. She sat propped up like a shop dummy in front of me, her eyes directed at me but seeming to look straight through me.

I didn't know what she meant. I was eleven years old, and little girls didn't have babies. Only mammies had babies, and I wasn't a mammy.

I stared at my mammy and didn't know what to say. My lips felt as if they were stuck together. The room was swirling around me. I still felt sick, and the mere thought that I was having a baby made me feel sicker still.

How could a baby get inside my tummy? My tummy wasn't big enough to have a baby in it. It wasn't big and round like Mammy's was when I pushed my ear up to it to listen for baby Michael's heartbeat.

Mammy began to speak again as I stood in front of her, dumbstruck. This time her voice was angry.

'You're a freak,' she blurted out. 'Your baby will be disabled.'

I knew it was real now, and what Mammy was saying was true. I didn't understand anything at all about having babies. I didn't want to have a baby. A tear ran down my cheek. I really didn't want to have a disabled baby. I didn't grasp what any of it really meant, but her words frightened me to death. I imagined I had some scary monster inside me, not comprehending how it got there or how it might go away.

Mammy snapped me out of my thoughts, pushing me on to the single bed, shouting very loudly, 'D'you hear me? You're a freak! Stay up here until I say!'

She pulled the thick curtains tightly across the black blanket on the window.

'Stay up here, you freak! I don't want anyone to see you.'

I heard Mammy stamp downstairs, leaving me sprawled on the bed, wide-eyed with shock.

I couldn't believe I was having a baby and that I was a freak, and my baby would be disabled, whatever that meant.

I thought about singing in school, and how happy I was in my new class. What would happen now? Would I have to stay locked in this room until the baby came, or would Mammy take me to hospital, like she did when Margaret had Theresa? I'm a freak. I'm having a baby. The baby will be a freak. Those words spun around in my head.

I loved babies. I loved all the beautiful newborn babies I

had seen, but I didn't want to have a baby myself. And if I had to have a baby, I didn't want one who was a freak. It wasn't fair.

I hardly slept that night, even though Daddy didn't go anywhere near me. I had scary dreams about ugly monsters. I was trapped in a big witch's cauldron with lots of scaly monsters, and they were kicking me all over.

The next morning, I went to school as normal. Mammy was fast asleep when I woke up, and Daddy had gone to work, so I sorted out the little ones and took myself to school, with thoughts about the baby nagging away inside me.

I was pleased to be out of the house and happy I wasn't going to be locked in the bedroom until the baby came. I didn't know how long the wait would be, and I didn't want to be stuck in the house for days, or years, or however long it might be before the baby appeared.

I didn't know how babies were made or how they arrived. Maybe it would be like Mother Dorothy said. Maybe I would go up a lane and come back pushing a pram?

I didn't tell my friends I was having a baby. I wanted them to be my friends and sing and dance with me and watch my little comedy shows. I wanted everything to stay the way it was before the baby was in my tummy.

From then on, whenever I felt the kicks, I ignored them. If I felt sick, I didn't say anything. My tummy started to get a lot bigger than normal, but I just put up with it. What else could I do?

I had horrible thoughts about the thing inside me, and how scary it looked. I was afraid it might kill me as it banged about inside me. What was it doing to my insides? Some days, I wondered if having a baby in my stomach was like when you had a bug in your stomach. Maybe it would just go one day, and suddenly I would get better? I thought that would be the best thing.

Mammy would be pleased about that too, because she was very angry about the baby. She was shouting at me all the time, calling me a freak every time she looked at me. I wondered if I was turning into a monster like the baby. Maybe that was why Mammy kept calling me a freak.

She was fighting with Daddy every night too, but when he came upstairs to bed, swearing and cursing after being kicked and slapped by Mammy, Daddy ignored me. It was as if he was terrified of even brushing against me.

It was winter, and when the snow came I wasn't allowed to go outside, because Mammy said she was afraid I would fall.

One Friday night, all the neighbours and the children off the street were out playing in the snow. I watched out the window when Daddy came home with the housekeeping money. Someone threw a snowball at him, so he went into our backyard and got his work shovel.

Our neighbour was hiding behind his wall, and my dad threw a shovelful of snow over the wall at him.

I saw everyone enjoying themselves, running in and out of

the gardens and laughing. It was so unusual for Daddy to join in the fun.

I felt so envious and left out, I cried. I didn't want to be stuck inside with Mammy. It was as if I was in trouble for having the freak inside me. I didn't know why Mammy was worried about me falling. She had never worried about me hurting myself before.

I craved milk all the time and kept drinking it, but that night Mammy wouldn't let me have milk with my dinner.

She told me if I drank milk, my boobs would get bigger and 'people would notice'. I was so upset I sobbed again. I hated being different, it was horrible. I just wanted to play in the snow and drink milk like all the other children.

After that, Mammy started hiding milk from me, and one morning I felt so desperate to drink a glass I got up early and stole a pint from the neighbour's doorstep.

On another morning, I crept downstairs early to try to find some milk before Mammy hid it, and was delighted to find a bottle standing on the kitchen table.

I grabbed it quickly and gulped it down greedily, but the second it hit my throat I started to retch. It tasted disgusting, and it was full of big slimy lumps. I staggered back upstairs, retching and heaving, to find Mammy laughing her head off in her bed.

'That'll teach you to rob the milk,' she wheezed. She told me she had hidden that bottle for a week so it would go sour and teach me a lesson. It did, and I felt very ill all day and couldn't face drinking milk again for a long time afterwards.

I started skipping school because I felt so ill, and Mammy seemed pleased. She never told me off for having days off. I think she liked having me in the house so I could help sweep the floor and wash out the babies' nappies.

I didn't look at my body to see what was happening. I had never really looked at my own body. Mammy always told me I was a 'dirty bitch' if I looked at her by accident when she was getting dressed. I didn't want to be a dirty bitch and look at myself, so I never did.

I threw my clothes on in the dark in the morning and took them off in the dark at night, as always. Besides, I was too scared to look.

A few weeks later, Mother Dorothy marched into our classroom with a face like thunder.

'Cynthia Murphy, I want to talk to you in my office!' she boomed.

I blushed. Did she know I was a freak, and was she going to shout at me for being so weird?

I dutifully followed her into her office, head bowed and hands clasped across my belly.

'Are you pregnant, child?' she demanded. 'No, Mother Dorothy, of course I'm not pregnant!' I replied, shocked and insulted by the question. Mammy hadn't used the word 'pregnant'. How dare Mother Dorothy say I was pregnant?

Thoughts dashed through my head. Thank goodness she

hadn't asked me if I was having a freak, because then I would have had to lie.

I wasn't pregnant like Mammy and Margaret got pregnant. I wasn't a mammy having a baby. I was having a monster, but I wasn't telling Mother Dorothy that. Mammy had warned me to say nothing to the nuns and had threatened to beat me if I did, so I just denied everything.

Mammy was so keen to keep the secret that she had started telling me to hide upstairs if anyone came to the door. Daddy had been angrier than ever lately too, and had threatened me with a thrashing many times.

I didn't know why, because he didn't seem to know about the monster. He never mentioned it like Mammy did. But if I told Mother Dorothy and she came knocking on the door, he would beat me for sure.

My legs already felt sore all the time. I didn't want Daddy thrashing them with his belt and making them hum with pain. I could never sit down properly for ages after he whacked the back of my thighs, and I wanted to sit down all the time now.

There was no way I was telling Mother Dorothy my secret. 'No, Mother Dorothy,' I repeated firmly. 'I certainly am not pregnant!' My cheeks were burning. I was horrified.

I would never have told her my secret in a million years. Mother Dorothy had beaten me for having lice in my hair. What would she do to me if I had a freak in my tummy?

'Then why do you keep wearing that smock coat to school

every day?' she demanded. 'And why will you not take it off in the classroom?'

It was true. I had been wearing a three-quarter-length smock jacket every day for a couple of months now. I suppose it stood out because it had big buttons down the front, but my own coat didn't fit me any more.

Mammy ordered me to wear the coat to school every day to hide my tummy, and so I did. I also wore a floaty dress sometimes, because it flowed over my tummy and wasn't as tight as my other clothes.

My chest was getting bigger now too. Mammy hadn't given me a bra, and I only had an old vest to wear and felt embarrassed by my changing shape, so I was happy to hide under the coat.

'Take the coat off,' ordered Mother Dorothy. 'Remove that coat immediately!'

I was terrified of Mother Dorothy and what she might do if my secret came out, so I shook my head and refused point blank.

Mammy had told me I had to wear the coat all day, that I was to hide the freak in my tummy. The very last thing I wanted was for Mother Dorothy to know my secret, or for anyone to see the funny new shape of my body.

'Take off the coat,' she barked again.

I couldn't take the coat off. My legs and arms were still skinny like they always were, but my tummy was swollen and sticking out. I knew, I could feel it.

I fiddled with one of the big plastic buttons on the front

of the jacket. There was no way I could take the coat off. It would cause so much trouble.

I burst into tears and darted straight out of Mother Dorothy's office.

I dreaded going to school the next day, and made up my mind that when Mother Dorothy spoke to me again I would say absolutely nothing. It must be a terrible sin to have a monster in your tummy, and I couldn't face a caning. I had to stay silent.

I sighed with great relief when Mother Dorothy said I was to sit with my back to the rest of the class. I said nothing and just did it, very relieved not to have a scene in front of my classmates.

The next time my friends asked me to go swimming at the pool down at Saville Park, I just said no. I loved swimming and missed our trips there at the weekend, but Mammy wouldn't let me go and, besides, I didn't want anyone to see my bulging stomach, so I made excuses. If any of my classmates asked about my smock coat, I told them I had pneumonia and had to stay warm, because Mammy had told me that was what I should say, and it was winter, after all.

Mammy was the only one who really knew what was happening, so I did everything Mammy told me to do. She was my mammy, and she knew about babies. She was the only one who could really help me, so I followed her orders and didn't complain or ask any questions that might make her angry with me. I needed her to help me, even though I felt very uneasy around her.

She still took me up to the building though. She gave me whiskey or sherry first, to make me 'feel better'. Sometimes I had so much I felt very dizzy. My mind was spinning and I couldn't think about anything, but I did hear some of the men talking about my shape.

It was as if I was only half there, but I could clearly hear them saying things about my big chest and round tummy.

They said they liked it, but I wondered why. I thought I looked horrible, because I felt horrible, but they seemed to like it a lot. They wanted to touch me more. I was very glad Mammy gave me the alcohol. I didn't want to be there at all, and in a way I wasn't.

Mammy stuffed the bundle of money in her pocket as usual and helped me walk home. My legs ached and my ankles felt squishy and bloated. I wanted to be sick and I wobbled when I walked. I would never have made it home without Mammy. I needed my mammy, but her presence still made me scared and confused. Why was she putting me though all this? I wanted it to stop. Maybe Mammy would make it stop now I was having a baby?

Chapter 14

Noleen

It was Tuesday, 3 April 1973, and I was eleven and a half years old. The Easter holidays were coming up and I was looking forward to getting an Easter egg.

Mammy and Daddy sometimes left eggs at the ends of our beds, and we all gobbled them down as soon as we woke up, knowing that, if we didn't, somebody else would.

I went to school as normal that day, sitting at the back facing the wall, wearing my smock coat, with Mother Dorothy looking down at me.

I was glad the holidays were coming up, and I wondered how long this thing would go on for. I wished the baby in my tummy would just go away, and then I could go swimming again with my friends, and Mammy would stop calling me a freak.

I wanted to ask Mammy some questions, but I was frightened to. Every time she looked at me lately she scowled and shouted or slapped my face sharply, so I said nothing.

'My friend is coming over tonight, Cynthia,' Mammy told me at bedtime. 'You're to go in the back bedroom with him.'

Each time I heard those words I wanted the ground to swallow me up. I knew who that was going to be. It was that awful thug.

The last time he came over he punched me in the face and laughed when I cried. He hurt my tummy when he forced himself on me. I was worn out tonight and just wanted to sleep. I always prayed he would stagger in and fall asleep on the bed so I could be left in peace. But he never did. It would be the usual chaos and violence and sheer terror.

I lay in bed panicking. I couldn't hide behind the door or under the bed like I had sometimes. My tummy was too big, and my legs ached so much I needed to lie down.

I needed the toilet too, and before Mammy's friend came in from the pub I crept downstairs cautiously in the dark.

Feeling my way across the backyard and into the outside toilet, I stepped cautiously through the old wooden door.

As soon as my feet hit the cold concrete of the toilet floor I wet myself. I sat down on the toilet feeling shaken. I'd never wet myself like that before, and it startled me.

My stomach was feeling tight and sore, and I felt weird inside. I had a strange sensation down below too, like something pushing down inside me. It scared me. I wanted my mammy.

I crept inside and went up to Mammy in her chair by the fire.

'Mammy, I'm sorry,' I blurted out. 'Mammy, I've wet on the toilet floor. My stomach is sore and...'

Mammy jumped out of her chair, fetched a light bulb and went outside to put it in the toilet. I scuttled after her, thinking it was odd, because we hardly ever had a bulb in the toilet, and Mammy never normally leapt out of her chair like that.

She looked at the floor, and so did I. Now I was even more confused. I hadn't just wet myself, there was watery-coloured blood on the floor. It frightened me, and I thought Mammy would shout, but she just told me to go into the sitting room and sit by the fire. I sat staring into the fire, feeling mesmerized by the dancing flames.

I knew that Daddy was in the house as I had heard him earlier with Mammy. But it was just Mammy's voice I heard now. She was muttering under her breath. I blinked sharply, peeling my gaze away from the fire.

I overheard Mammy's whispered words: 'We will have to kill her as well as the baby, we will have to kill her in case she tells what happened.'

I looked at the flames dancing in the fire, and heard the words dance in my head. They were all jumbled up and didn't make sense.

Then it all went very quiet until, moments later, Mammy reappeared. 'Go upstairs to bed,' she commanded.

I crept up into the front bedroom, the weight of my tummy slowing me down. I felt very relieved Mammy had stopped hissing and muttering. She had threatened me with all kinds of things in the past, and I knew she didn't want to actually kill me – did she?

Daddy was in the double bed, and I sat on the floor at the end of it, hunched in the alcove carved in the wall.

And that's when the pain started.

It got so sharp so quickly I started whimpering and writhing in agony.

I sat there for ages clenching my tummy, and the pain was so bad I couldn't help making noises, even though I was afraid of Mammy getting cross. I thought I was going to die.

Daddy stirred and sat up in bed when Mammy entered the room. Now they were shouting at each other.

'Get her!' he was yelling. 'Get her, will you!'

He wanted Mammy to stop me writhing and screaming, but I couldn't stop. The pain was coming faster and faster, tightening my stomach and making me push down below.

It was unbearable. I winced and pushed. It felt like I could push the pain out, and suddenly I was groaning and the pain was nearly out.

The baby was on the floor.

Mammy picked it up, but I barely even looked. I was still in agony and still pushing. There was something else inside me.

Mammy clawed at me, trying to pull out the rest of it. Her touch frightened me. She was touching me between the legs, pulling something out of me, hurting me with her spiky finger-nails.

'Daddy!' I screamed. Mammy was hurting me. I didn't like her touching me down there. I wanted her to stop.

Mammy had it now. She pulled it out of me. It was big a lump of blood and veins. I recoiled when I saw it. I was still twisting in agony. I was panic-stricken by this thing that had come out of me. I had no idea what it was. Maybe it really was a freak? It scared me so much.

Daddy appeared above me. He looked stern and incensed. He handed Mammy a pair of scissors and one of her knitting needles.

'I don't want them – you do it,' he warned her.

Mammy thrust them back at Daddy, but he shoved them back in her face.

They were arguing now, hissing and snarling over who would 'do it'. I was petrified. The blade of the scissors and the point of the needle dangled in front of me, terrifying me.

I didn't know what they wanted to do, I was just glad to have Daddy here, so I wasn't all alone with Mammy. She was frightening me far more than he was. She usually did.

Eventually Mammy said, 'If you won't do it, then I will,' and she snatched the scissors and the knitting needle out of his outstretched hand.

It was dark in the room, but I could see the baby now. It was on the floor in front of me. I could see it was a baby girl. She wasn't a monster after all. She was a perfect baby girl, with soft hair and pink skin. Her little fingers were wriggling, and I wanted to reach out and touch her, but I was frozen with shock.

Mammy was reaching for her now. She had the knitting needle.

I saw it flash as she lifted it above my baby's face. I wanted to scream but nothing came out. I was afraid of making Mammy any angrier. I was afraid of what was going to happen.

I looked on in helpless horror as she stabbed the needle into my baby's beautiful little face.

She did it once, and then she did it over and over again. She stabbed her in the neck too.

I could hardly breathe through my shock. My baby's face wasn't perfect any more.

She was bleeding, but just a moment ago she had been so flawless. I couldn't take it in.

Daddy was watching Mammy, but started to tut and shake his head, like he was in a hurry. He walked away, and I heard him sink back into bed.

I had to touch my baby. I had to feel her warm skin.

I stretched out my trembling hand and nearly reached her, but Mammy jabbed the top of my hand sharply with the knitting needle.

It hurt, and I pulled back.

'If you ever tell anyone about this, you are next,' she spat.

'Please, Mammy,' I stuttered. 'Please let me touch my baby.'

'Shut up!' she snarled. 'Just shut up!'

I really wanted to touch my baby. I felt an overpowering

urge to reach out again, but Mammy's hand swiped out in front of me.

She had the scissors in her hand now. It looked like she was going to cut the bloody rope that was hanging out of the baby's tummy, but then Mammy paused, and just ripped it out of my baby instead.

The baby cried, and Mammy put her on the pink double candlewick bedspread off Daddy's bed and left the room with her.

I couldn't move. My body felt very heavy, and my eyes started to go black. I was slipping away, blacking out with pain.

Everything went very dark, and when I opened my eyes I tried to move, but my legs felt paralysed. It felt as if I'd lain there for a while, but I wasn't sure how long.

I blinked and looked down slowly. I saw three leather belts strapped around my legs, pressing them tightly together.

The pain in my tummy was back again, as sharp as ever. My whole body was aching, and I started to cry. I couldn't lift my legs, I was in too much pain. I reached down and undid the buckles on the belts. Blood was running down my legs. All of a sudden, my mind slipped into a sharper focus for a second. I had to go down the stairs and out the front door.

I'd never experienced such fear in my life. It felt so raw, as if the fear was in every part of my body and running through my veins like poison, jolting me and terrifying me.

Cynthia Owen

I had to get out. I had to get away. I was in a blind panic now.

I inched down the stairs in agony and reached out ever so slowly for the front door.

I prised it open carefully and breathed in a drop of the night air, smelling freedom.

But before I could get out of the house, Mammy was yelling at me like a maniac from the hall. 'Get back here!' she screamed. I was so afraid of her that I closed the door instantly and walked obediently into the sitting room.

Mammy turned her back and walked away from me.

She was moving towards the sink, and she had the baby in her arms.

The baby was still in the pink blanket, and she was covered in blood. I started screaming hysterically.

I was shocked to see that Granny was at the back of the living room. She was standing at the kitchen table with her hand on her hip.

'I told you not to do it in front of her,' she scolded.

'Put the baby in the sink and wash the blood off it.'

Then Granny looked at me. 'Cynthia, sit on the blanket on the floor.'

It was the crochet blanket that was usually thrown over the back of my granny's chair.

The armchair had been moved back, and the crochet blanket was in its space.

'Sit there,' Granny ordered.

I slumped onto the blanket.

Mammy was at the sink now. I looked up and panicked. She wasn't washing the baby at all. She was stabbing her again and again in the neck.

The baby was crying and wriggling.

'Try the gas oven,' Granny said to Mammy.

I watched horror-struck as Mammy placed the baby on a green towel on the draining board and turned on the oven.

I waited for her to light it, because that's what always happened after the gas was switched on. But Mammy didn't light it.

She placed the baby's head by the oven door. The baby was still crying and squirming.

Her little body wasn't pretty and pink any more. She was starting to turn blue.

I was weeping loudly now, and complaining that the smell of the gas was choking me and hurting my head.

Mammy was on her knees in front of the oven.

I watched helplessly as she moved her own head and body away from the gas fumes but held my baby at the oven door.

Granny walked to the back door and opened it, letting some gas out of the room.

Mammy rushed outside with the baby. Granny was distracted, and nobody was looking at me, so I seized my chance and staggered out the back door and locked myself in the outside toilet.

I sat down on the toilet seat, panting and puffing and trying to gather my thoughts.

I put my hand down the side of the toilet towards the floor to get some paper to wipe myself, and my hand touched something soft and furry.

I snatched my arm away in terror and ran back into the house screaming.

'Mammy, please help! Mammy, there is something furry in the toilet!'

'Cynthia, love, it's our neighbour's rabbit,' she snapped back.

But I knew our neighbour didn't have a rabbit. When I argued, Mammy got angry and started to shout at me, and I suddenly realized that it must have been my baby in the toilet, dumped on the floor.

I dashed back out, slammed the toilet door behind me and picked my baby up off that cold, damp concrete.

I hugged her to my chest, but something frightened me. It felt like I was holding a slab of meat in my arms, because the baby felt so cold.

Was this really my baby? I was in such a state I wasn't sure.

Mammy came to the toilet door and told me to come out now. I didn't move or speak, even when she started to bang loudly on the door.

'Come out here and get away from that baby,' she bellowed.

'No, I just want to hold her,' I shouted back. 'Leave me alone.'

Then suddenly I felt so scared I walked out of the toilet,

holding my baby. I just wanted to hold her, that's what mattered most. Mammy lunged at me and grabbed the baby out of my arms.

She told me to follow her into the house and sit down on the crocheted blanket that was still on the floor. As soon as I sat down on the blanket, Mammy told me to get off it and pass it to her.

I was terrified, so I did as I was told. Mammy placed the baby on the blanket and laid her face down, on her stomach. Then she started ranting at me. I couldn't take in what she was saying at first. It was a stream of pure anger, and Mammy was stabbing the baby again, plunging the knitting needle into the back of her neck.

The baby wasn't moving, but Mammy turned her over and carried on stabbing her again and again in the neck, and once in the chin. She had a dimpled chin, like my Daddy.

'You should have listened to me and kept away from him,' she accused.

'It's all your fault, Cynthia! I told you to keep away from him, but you would not listen, would you?' I just knew she meant Daddy, I could tell.

Mammy's pale skin was scarlet, and she was panting and gasping for breath.

She seemed worn out from the effort of stabbing the baby, but she kept stabbing.

'Now will you listen to me?' she taunted. 'Now will you keep away from him?'

I sat, terrorized, on the floor, rocking back and forth, saying the same thing over and over again.

'That's my baby, I want that baby. That's my baby, I want that baby.'

As I watched Mammy stabbing and shouting, I felt as if I was looking out of a window that had misted over. I could see what was happening in front of me, but only through the blurred cloud of my mind.

My head felt heavy, as if someone had poured cement into it and it was beginning to harden.

'I'll teach you to listen to me in future,' she seethed. 'Now look what you've made me do, all because you wouldn't listen to me.'

With every rant she stabbed my baby in the neck and face again. The baby was dead, I could see that. She had stopped moving and crying, but still Mammy carried on stabbing her viciously.

It reminded me of the times when she beat me.

Now she was doing the same thing to my baby, and I was as powerless as when Mammy beat me. I was a child too.

'Get the laundry bag out of the cupboard,' she ordered.

I had to crawl along the floor to the cupboard because I was in so much pain I could no longer stand up. I gave her the big green laundry bag, which we hardly ever used, then I told Mammy I wanted to go to the toilet again.

When I got outside I noticed a plastic bag on the coals in the coal shed, and for a moment I thought my baby might be hidden inside it, so I started to try to stretch my hand out over the coals to grab the bag.

My stomach hit off the little wall that kept the coal in, and I cried out in pain. It made me think that my baby had been safely inside me, and now she was dead. I couldn't think of anything else but hiding, so I dashed back into the toilet. I knew there was a bolt on the door, and I desperately wanted to lock myself in, to be all alone.

I thought that if I was on my own I could escape the horrors of the night, but once I was inside, alone in the dark, I became hysterical and lost control of myself completely.

I screamed out loud to Mammy over and over again: 'I want my baby. I'll get you back for what you've done. I'll get you back one day. You'll see!'

I didn't care who heard me. I wasn't bothered what anyone might think or do. Suddenly I was no longer afraid, other things mattered more. My baby mattered more.

I exhausted myself by screaming and wailing and shouting threats. I was dead beat, and after a while I could say no more. I was trembling with nerves and fear and my body was pulsating with pain.

Now all I wanted was to go back into the warm house so I could feel better.

I hoped I would be allowed to go to bed and fall to sleep, but Mammy told me we were going out for a walk. I didn't want to go out for a walk, but Mammy already had her coat on, and I could tell we were going whether I liked it or not.

Chapter 15

Goodbye

Mammy had the bag with my baby in it.

I followed her silently out of the back door and down the side passage, wondering what we were going to do so late. I didn't know what time it was, but it was deep into the night, or even the early hours of the morning. There was a chill in the air. Everything was very black and silent, and I felt scared and cold.

I followed Mammy blindly for ages, feeling deadened with pain and shock. After a while I realized we were walking down a side road towards the main bus route in Sandycove.

Mammy was still carrying the laundry bag in her hand.

'Cross here with me,' she told me. 'If we're on the other side of the road, the police cars going to Dalkey won't see us.'

We walked on to the pier in Sandycove, and Mammy told me to go down on to the long slipway that led from the pier into the water.

I obeyed. I couldn't think properly for myself, so I listened to Mammy. It was dark, and I was scared, so I did what she told me. As always, I was too frightened to disobey her.

'Bend down and see if you can see an old pram in the water,' Mammy said in a coaxing voice. 'We could get it out and take it home with us.'

I bent down to try to see the pram in the dark water, and Mammy strode up behind me. Before I could turn round to look at her I was falling.

She had shoved me really hard, and I was falling through the water.

It was ice-cold and my heart jolted with shock. I gasped for air but swallowed salty mouthfuls of water as I kicked my legs furiously and tried to push myself back up to the surface.

I'd plunged so deeply into the freezing water that I'd hit the bottom of the sea bed. I kicked again and my legs hit something.

It felt like concrete, and I managed to get my feet on it and stand up. I could see again now. It was the part of the slipway that was sunk in the water, and I started wading up it, fighting for breath and shivering with cold. Then I heard another loud splash, and I looked up to see the green bag floating on top of the swirling, dark sea in front of me.

I screamed hysterically and started lunging desperately towards the laundry bag. It was slippery and heavy, but I managed to grab it and clutched it to my chest.

I tried to make my way back to Mammy, further up the

slipway. I felt frozen to the bone now, and I was stinging and throbbing with pain in my stomach and legs.

'Follow me!' she growled angrily. We kept walking and went down some steps, and as we got to the last step, I put my foot down on to the path and felt something crunch under my foot.

I looked down in horror. There were hundreds of bugs scampering about everywhere. They terrified me, and I started to scream, but Mammy told me to shut up and hurry up. The bugs had just come out because it was raining, she said.

I shut my mouth firmly, because Mammy was losing her temper, and I followed her into the little park in Sandycove, where she told me I had to put the bag down under the bushes. But I wasn't going to let go of that bag for anything. I was scared of Mammy, but this was my baby. She grabbed my arm and dragged me back towards the sea again.

We walked on a bit more and went down a lane I'd never been down before. It led us out on to the 'metals', which was a lane running from Dalkey to Dun Laoghaire.

We had to cross an old railway bridge to get onto the 'metals'. The bridge scared me. It looked so old and rusty I was sure it would crash to the ground as soon as we stepped on to it.

'Hurry up,' Mammy hassled. She was already in the middle of the bridge. 'Hurry up!'

I trod as lightly as I could and edged my way along. When I reached the middle where Mammy was, she pointed over the edge.

'Climb up there and see if you can see any trains coming,' she told me.

I could see if a train was coming by looking through the wire mesh on the bridge. I didn't need to climb up, and I was too frightened to.

'No, Mammy,' I said, but she wouldn't take no for an answer. 'Please, Mammy, no. I don't want to. I'm frightened I'll fall.'

I stood my ground and didn't go up, so Mammy grabbed the laundry bag from me and we carried on walking, turning left up a side road that led us up into Dun Laoghaire town, where we ended up at the Christian Institute.

It was an old red-brick building, and Mammy had told me that, years ago, it used to be a library and she went to dances there with Daddy when they were dating.

She walked up the steps of the building saying she wondered if she could still see the dance floor through the window. She made me look through a side window, but I had to lean over to see in, and my stomach hurt. I turned to tell Mammy my tummy was hurting and saw a police car driving towards us. It was slowing down, and I knew it was going to stop.

'Mammy,' I hissed. She was peering though the big front gates of the Institute.

'Mammy, the police are here.' The car was pointing towards Dalkey, and pulled up in front of us. There were two policemen inside.

'Are you all right, ladies?' one of them asked.

'Yes, Officer. We are just on our way home from visiting

relatives,' Mammy answered, before turning on her heels and walking off in the opposite direction to Dalkey.

I started to walk off in front of Mammy and she pulled me back.

'Walk on the outside of the pavement near to the road,' she said. 'And keep the bag between us.'

'Where are we going, Mammy?' I asked. 'What are we doing?'

She told me we were going to see a furniture shop that belonged to a friend of Daddy's.

We passed by the old cinema house called the Adelphi, which had been boarded off. Mammy told me she went to the cinema with Daddy when they were courting. 'Look through the fencing to see if the cinema has been knocked down yet,' she told me. I was relieved now that Mammy wasn't angry with me. She was reminiscing, as I'd heard her do so many times. I knew it wasn't really like any other night, because we had the bag, and the baby was in the bag. But I didn't want to spoil Mammy's mood. It was better if she was remembering the 'good old days', as she called them. I felt less afraid.

I wondered how long I would have to walk for. My tummy was knotted up with pain and each step made me wince, but I kept going and didn't grumble.

We turned left into Corrig Avenue, then right into a dark lane way. Mammy told me this was Lee's Lane, and that the furniture shop was up there.

Soon she stopped outside a shop that had wire mesh on the windows.

'Look inside at the furniture,' Mammy told me. I tried, but it was pitch-black in the lane way, and darker still inside the shop.

I sensed Mammy slip away. When I turned round, she was walking off into the night. I felt afraid of being left there all alone, but I didn't know what to do, so I just stood still.

Moments later, I was relieved to see her rushing back. She was breathing heavily and telling me to hurry up, because we had to go. I felt her take hold of my arm. She was marching me out of the lane now, into the light of the street.

I could see better now, and I realized Mammy wasn't holding the laundry bag any more.

'Mammy! You've left the bag in the lane way!' I cried.

'Shall I go back and get it for you?'

'No, Cynthia. Keep walking. There's nothing in there we need.'

But I knew my baby was in the bag, and I knew she had left her in the lane way. I didn't want Mammy getting mad though. I didn't want her to shout or hit me. But at the same time I didn't want to leave my baby all alone.

I rushed off into the blackness before she could stop me.

I saw the furniture shop and turned left into another part of the lane, the part where I guessed Mammy had run off with the bag.

There was a gateway in front of me. I looked in the alcove, and there was the bag, wrapped up tightly.

I recognized it and knew I had to look inside.

Opening the bag carefully, I saw my baby's body and wanted to touch her, but before I could reach out to her Mammy was snatching the bag away from me.

'Put that down and come with me!' she snapped, dumping the bag back in the alcove and dragging me out of the lane.

'I've seen the baby in the bag!' I sobbed. 'Let me go, Mammy! I've seen her. I've seen my baby in the bag!'

Mammy was blazing with fury now, dragging me brutally down the lane while I cried hysterically, trying to pull away from her with all my might.

'Let me go back and get my baby! Please, Mammy, let me go back and get my baby!'

'No, Cynthia,' she wheezed. She had a bad chest and was coughing and spluttering with the effort of dragging me along.

'It's for the best. You will never have to suffer again. It is all over now. Once the baby is found it will put an end to it.'

She was talking about Daddy and all the men who hurt me and what they did to me, I was sure of it, but I didn't care about the men right now. All I cared about was my baby.

'Please, Mammy,' I pleaded. 'I have to go to her. Let me go back and get my baby, I beg you.'

She slapped me hard across the face and I slumped to the ground, exhausted and weak with pain, and sobbing uncontrollably.

A man came walking towards me and asked if I was OK. 'She's a gypsy and has been drinking,' I heard Mammy say in a pitiful voice.

He left us alone and went on his way. I had to get back to that lane, I just had to be with my baby.

'Mammy,' I sobbed. 'Nobody will find the baby where you left her. Why don't you let me put her in a more open place?'

Mammy thought for a moment, then agreed. She pointed to a streetlamp in the distance, told me to put the baby under there and meet her on the main road.

I felt very alone and frightened walking up that dark lane. As soon as I felt the bag in my hands again I knew I wasn't going to put my baby under the streetlamp. It was what Mammy had told me to do and I didn't want to obey Mammy any more, but I did want my baby to be found. I hated the thought of her lying there alone in the dark.

Maybe I could put her on the main road? No, it seemed too dangerous.

Something told me to look inside the bag again, to say goodbye. I started opening it and reached gently inside, because I wanted to touch her when I said goodbye. I felt her inside the bag, and it was such a shock. She seemed so cold. She needed to be wrapped up warm.

I walked back along the lane to get some newspapers to wrap her in. I'd seen them in the lane earlier.

I gathered them up and went back to the bag. I started to place the newspaper around her as gently as I could.

As I did so, I heard something fall out of the bag. It was a knitting needle. I gasped, and then something else in the bag caught my eye.

It was the bloody lump that came out of me after the baby. It looked disgusting, and it terrified me. There were sanitary towels in there too.

I wanted to say goodbye now. I wrapped the newspapers around the lower part of my baby's body and I said it, my heart aching with sadness. 'Although I have to leave you alone in this lane way, I will take you with me in my heart.' I said the words in my head, and I told myself that I would pretend that I had picked her up and taken her with me in my arms. I wrapped the bag up as I had found it, bound up like a parcel. I didn't want Mammy to know I had opened it again.

I held the bag to me tightly, trying to cuddle my baby through the plastic, and then I sat with her for a long time, crying and talking to her. I told her that, someday, no matter how or when, I would get my Mammy for what she had done to my baby.

As I cried I kept asking the same question over and over again: 'How could you do this to me, Mammy?' I tried to peel myself away from the bag, but it was breaking my heart.

How could I leave her there alone? And what if she was never found? Would she lie there alone for ever?

I'd have to hide her now and come back for her the next day. 'I'll come back for you tomorrow,' I whispered.

Mammy would get impatient waiting for me, and she would punish me severely for taking so long. I had to go now, so I told the baby I was not leaving her for ever, I was just leaving her there for the night. I would come back and get her the next day, and take her home with me.

I decided to go back to the alcove and push the baby in the bag under the gateway to hide her. First I picked up the bag and the knitting needle and then put a few more newspapers on top of the baby to keep her warm.

When I saw the needle in my hand I shuddered. I felt sick at the thought of putting it anywhere near the baby, so I poked it into another bag of rubbish that was left beside the gateway.

My bag wouldn't fit under the gateway now, so I threw it over the wall and then felt instantly afraid, because I hadn't done exactly what Mammy had told me.

I looked up at the sky and noticed it was getting bright and the birds were singing. I panicked and ran out of the lane, hoping Mammy would not be too mad with me.

I ran in the direction she had told me to, and it brought me out opposite the Dun Laoghaire police station.

Mammy was nowhere in sight. I was angry that she had left me on my own, and I started running down the main road, calling out 'Mammy' until I spotted her in the distance.

She was furious I had taken so long, and I remained upset she had walked away, leaving me on my own.

We argued on and on, about the bag and the baby and Mammy leaving me on my own. I was eleven-years-old. I didn't want to be left in a strange lane way on my own. It scared me. I didn't want to leave my baby in the dimly-lit lane way on her own either. It didn't seem fair at all. I felt so very sorry for her, lying in the dark inside the bag, all alone without a mammy.

The arguments went on, and the walking went on. My whole body ached. I longed for my bed, and when I finally got there I collapsed, my mind and body drained and battered.

It was evening time again when I woke up, because I could smell the dinner cooking.

I was tied to the single bed, with nylon stockings holding my wrists to the bedposts.

I started screaming, and Mammy appeared at the doorway.

She told me my baby had been found, because she had heard it on the news.

'Shut up and come downstairs for your dinner,' she said in the next breath. Untying my hands, she added, 'Act as if nothing has happened.'

I did as I was told. I didn't know what else I could do, and I didn't have a drop of energy left in my body for a fight.

The evening passed in a blurry haze. I heard the little ones in the house cry and chatter as normal, and I saw Mammy sit in the rocking chair and drink as usual, while Daddy was in the pub.

I tried to act normal too, and I think I did a good job, because nobody asked me anything about what happened the day before.

The next morning, I got the younger ones dressed and fed and myself ready for school. Mammy came down and handed me a packet of thick sanitary towels and a sanitary belt. I'd never seen a belt like it before, and Mammy explained how to use it, to keep the towel in place in my knickers.

My tummy felt all wobbly and sore, and when I looked in the mirror I was shocked. I looked like I hadn't slept for a month, and my clothes were hanging off me.

At school I acted as normal as possible though, and nobody asked what was wrong with me or why I'd missed the previous day. It was a typical, unremarkable school day. We did sums and read books, and I was very surprised by that.

Inside, I felt very different, like I had never felt before. I was burning up with fury and fear, and I had lots of dark thoughts smouldering in my brain.

I didn't trust Mammy at all any more, and I wasn't going to do as she told me. I hated her. I hated what she did to my baby. I hated how my baby looked in that bag, all wounded and covered in blood.

It wasn't right, and one day I would tell people what Mammy did to my baby. I would get Mammy for what she did.

When I was bigger and stronger I would get all the people who did bad things to me and my baby. I made a promise to both of us.

After I walked home from school that night there was a programme on television called *Garda Patrol*. It was relating the story of how the baby was found. I sat transfixed, hanging on every word but knowing I could say nothing.

It showed the laundry bag, and told how two eleven-year-old boys had found the baby on the way home from fishing. The presenter said that the mother of the child could be in need of urgent medical treatment, and this confused me.

If I urgently needed medical treatment, then why had I gone to school that day, and why was I now sitting watching the television?

I didn't understand what he was saying. He urged the mother of the baby to come forward. This made me angry.

I felt as if it was obvious who I was, and I wondered why I had to come forward. I was really tired, so why didn't they come and get me? Surely they knew who I was?

Mammy kept me off school for ages after that. I was locked up in our house for weeks, until well after the Easter holidays.

The days all merged into one. Mammy tried to act the same as ever, but she seemed agitated and nervous, and she shouted and watched the news all the time. Nobody mentioned the baby. Nobody came knocking on our door.

Daddy carried on like nothing had happened, still forcing me to 'get here now' in bed at night, even when I was still sore and bleeding.

It was as if everybody had forgotten about the baby, and what happened that night.

One day, I heard Mammy whispering with Granny. 'Are you talking about my baby?' I asked.

Mammy looked me straight in the eye. 'What baby?' she asked.

'You know what baby, Mammy. My baby. The baby we left in the laundry bag,' I said.

I started crying. It hurt me just to say the words.

'What baby?' Mammy asked me. 'There never was a baby. You're crazy, Cynthia, you're mad! Stop crying! Shut up!' Granny didn't argue or say anything to contradict Mammy.

It was the same every time I mentioned the baby. I was sure I wasn't mad, because the feeling in my heart never changed. I felt like I'd lost something, like a part of me was missing. I knew I'd had a baby and she had been taken away from me. I saw what Mammy did with my own eyes.

I would wake up during the night and my heart would be pounding. My arms would ache to hold my baby, and the feeling of emptiness was overbearing. I could hear my baby crying, and the sound haunted me and gave me terrible nightmares.

The more I mentioned the baby, the angrier Mammy got. I was much more frightened of her now than I had ever been, sure she was the one who was mad, not me, but as the months rolled by I started to get confused and forget things.

My memories dimmed, but Mammy's taunts that I was mad and talking rubbish got louder and clearer. Was there really a baby? I knew the truth. No nightmare could ever be that bad. My baby was real, but Mammy was never going to admit it. How could I ever get her back for what she did?

Chapter 16

The Fire

It was the dead of night, and I woke in terror to find Mammy clawing at my face. She was raking her long fingernails down my cheeks, calling me a 'little whore'.

I screamed out: 'Please, Mammy, no!' but she carried on scraping and cursing and scaring me.

I was so sleepy I felt barely alive.

'Please, please, no!' I cried. I lost all control and started lashing out at Mammy, begging her to stop.

She dragged me out of bed, and I sobbed when I realized she was taking me to the building.

My body was sore, and my head wasn't working properly at all. It was aching and pounding, and my limbs felt like lead weights. It was just weeks since I had the baby, and all I wanted to do was sleep.

Instead, I was subjected to another long night of torture in that creepy old building with those leering, disgusting men.

I now was more terrified than ever of those men in that building. Two of them had threatened me one day, telling me I'd be dead if I didn't keep my mouth shut. I knew they meant about the baby but, just like Mammy, they didn't admit it. Nobody talked about it, not really.

There was also a time when one of the men had even come to the house and taken me out in his car.

I begged Mammy not to make me go, but she pushed me out the door and told me to shut up.

'See how easy it is for me to get you on your own,' the man snarled. He drove me to a piece of wasteland and pointed to a desolate spot in the ground. 'If you don't keep quiet I'll bury you alive right there.'

When he brought me home I was shaking from head to toe. I was so scared I couldn't breathe properly, and I kept imagining that place he'd taken me to, and how terrifying it would be to be buried alive.

All I wanted to do was lie down, and I crawled upstairs, hoping for some peace and quiet.

Mammy was rampaging around the bedroom. I wanted to shut my eyes and get rid of the horrible thoughts in my head, but Mammy wouldn't let me.

She was tearing up anything of mine she laid her hands on – my clothes, some precious photos of my friends I had hidden in a drawer, and the few schoolbooks I owned.

'Please stop, Mammy!' I pleaded, but she didn't stop until she was gasping for air and looked utterly exhausted.

I thought she might be drunk, because she was swaying and slurring her words.

I'd heard Daddy yelling at her lately, telling her not to drink so much, but she had started sending me to the shop more than ever, asking me to buy a bottle of sherry.

Sometimes I refused because of what I heard Daddy say, and she flew at me in a fury, beating me in the face or smacking me with the wooden broomstick, then throwing me out of the house.

If I bought the sherry, Daddy belted me and called me a 'stupid cow'. I couldn't win, and I felt totally muddled by all the conflicts around me.

Mammy had started keeping me up late in the evenings a lot too. It was as if I was one of the grown-up children now. One night she was sitting by the fire drinking heavily and encouraging me to drink when she suddenly said, 'Watch me, Cynthia!'

Her eyes were rolling, and she took out a sharp sewing needle from her knitting bag.

'Watch me, Cynthia!' she said. 'Watch me kill myself!'

I screamed in shock. She was raking manically at her wrist with the needle, and blood began oozing from the cut.

'Mammy, please, no!' I cried. 'Please don't do that!'

I had to grab the needle off her and hide it while she ranted and raved and at last slumped into a drunken doze.

The sight of blood and the needle made me feel sick. I had

seen Mammy with blood and a needle before. I knew what she was capable of, and she terrified me.

I was too scared to go to bed in case Mammy cut herself again, but I didn't want to be downstairs when Daddy got in, or he would explode with rage. In the end I crept upstairs and lay in bed tossing and turning, petrified that Mammy might find the needle and kill herself.

After a while, Daddy came in drunk and fell fast asleep very quickly, but I still couldn't sleep a wink. I didn't want Mammy to kill herself. She scared me and I didn't like her, but she was still my mammy, and I didn't want her to die.

I crept back downstairs, and a horrible smell hit me the moment I walked in the sitting room.

It was gas. I'd smelled it that strongly once before, when Mammy had threatened to kill herself and had switched on the gas without lighting it. I never believed she really meant to do it though.

I ran to the kitchen to switch off the cooker, and jumped with fright. This time Mammy was lying slumped on the floor in front of the oven. The four gas rings and the oven were all fully switched on, but nothing was lit.

I could barely take it in. Mammy had really tried to kill herself, and all of us in our beds. I thought about the family upstairs. There were seven of us in total in the house that night. How could she?

I switched off the gas, opened the back door and tried to rouse her.

She was murmuring now, and I could see her cardigan rising and falling on her chest.

She wasn't dead. Thank God she wasn't dead.

The next day, I was furious and demanded an explanation. 'We would be better off dead,' was all Mammy said, over and over again. I felt so miserable I didn't care whether I lived or died, but I was outraged she might have killed my siblings in their beds. Who did she think she was?

I was twelve-years-old now, and in my last year of primary school. I never got a minute to myself, but I thought that was a good thing, because I liked to be busy.

If ever I did stop to think, horrible thoughts came into my head, and I didn't want to think horrible thoughts.

They confused me and frightened me, but I couldn't escape them. I had constant nightmares, but when I woke up screaming I couldn't tell myself it was all over and had just been a bad dream, because it wasn't.

In the dark at night, in the depths of my nightmares, I heard men's voices saying, 'She's my favourite!', 'Get over here, you!'

I could see Daddy with a nasty smile on his face, Mammy was cutting her wrist and lying with her head in the oven.

I woke up screaming and sweating so many times. The only relief I got was realizing nobody was actually touching me in my bed at that very moment, but then I'd lie there feeling terrified of what Mammy was doing downstairs.

I always went to check, and many times I caught her with the needle again, moaning she was 'better off dead'.

Mammy didn't do anything useful in the house at all now. She seemed to live in a world of her own, lying in bed or drinking endlessly in the chair.

Mary was now eight, Martin was six and Michael and Theresa were both two-years-old.

I loved my little brothers and sisters and did everything I could for them, washing and dressing them, feeding them and taking them out at the weekends to Sandycove or the park.

Martin finished school at twelve thirty, while my class worked on until two thirty, and Mammy made me sit Martin by my desk for those two hours, as he was too young to walk home alone and she wouldn't come and collect him.

I felt embarrassed having to mind him. It reminded me of when I'd first had to take him into class when he was two, when Mammy said she was sick. Now I knew she just couldn't be bothered to look after him.

I thought she was mean and selfish, but I didn't want Martin to suffer, so I let him sit with me, even though he distracted me in the classroom and the teacher shouted at me when I made mistakes because of him.

Some of the other girls rolled their eyes when he made a row or scratched his head, but they could look all they liked. He was my little brother and I was taking care of him. I'd toughened up, and I had far more things to worry about than what the other girls thought of me. I couldn't really care less about them.

Mammy never went out of the house in daylight now, and she didn't like it if I went out either. My friend Eileen asked me to go to the youth club with some other girls from the neighbourhood one night, and I begged Mammy to let me. I'd been before, with my big sisters, when they had been forced to drag me along even though I was too young, but I was old enough to go on my own now and I pleaded desperately with her to be able to go.

I was thrilled to bits when she agreed, and got myself dressed in my cleanest clothes and gave myself a good wash with a bucket of water I took upstairs to the bedroom. I even did my hair, making it look all blond and fluffy.

I heard the knock at the door and made my way downstairs, my heart racing with excitement. But it sank like a stone when I heard Mammy get there first.

'Fuck off! She's not comin' out!' she yelled, before slamming the door in my friend's face. I stood on the stairs burning with shame and anger, but Mammy burst out laughing, as if she'd played the best trick ever.

The following week she agreed that I really could go to the youth club, as long as I took Mary and Martin with me. I felt so desperate for a bit of fun and freedom I took them, and sat the pair of them in the corner with a bag of crisps while I chatted to my friends for a while, until the little ones got too bored. My friends didn't seem to care what Mammy was like, they didn't mention her or make any remarks at all. They were great for that.

The next day, I dawdled to school, sending the younger ones on ahead. That way I could get a few minutes' peace. I didn't care if I was late. I didn't care if my teacher made a show of me or sent me to Mother Dorothy to be caned. It was worth it to have some precious moments to myself.

The sun was breaking through a cloud and the birds were singing. It was spring 1974, and I was surviving. My teacher had a fit when I sauntered in. 'You're late!' she shouted, stating the obvious. 'So what?' I said back, shrugging my shoulders to show I didn't care.

Often I was late because I was busy sorting the little ones out on my own. There was nothing I could do about it. I didn't care if I got told off. Worse things could happen than being told off or threatened with a stick.

I knew that, and I pulled my hand away, as always, when Mother Dorothy stood me in front of Mr Greeny later that day and tried to 'teach me a lesson' for being persistently late and giving cheek. She could froth at the mouth and go purple and explode for all I cared. She couldn't kill me or lock me in prison, could she?

My friends loved it when I defied the teachers. I still got my work done, which seemed to irritate Mother Dorothy no end. I was learning, I was having a laugh and I was surviving, that's what mattered to me. There was a dark memory box in my head somewhere, full of lots of horrid thoughts. I could feel it lodged at the back in a very black corner, but I didn't ever want to bring it out into the light. Lots of men were still hurting me. I couldn't stop them, but nobody could force me to think about the baby and how she died, could they?

I didn't want to keep thinking about her. It made me too sad and confused. It was best to try and think about other things – but my plan didn't last for long.

On 11 March 1974, I was lying awake in the front bedroom. It was late at night and Daddy was in the double bed across the room. He still terrorized me every night, whether he touched me and hurt me or whether he fell fast asleep. Just being in the same room as him disgusted and frightened me, and I never, ever had a good night's sleep, even when he was snoring soundly.

I was on alert all the time, and tonight I was wide awake and listening to Peter outside, shouting goodnight to his friend Derek. Derek was my good friend Margaret's brother, and their family lived just down the road.

A short while later, I heard a loud bang, followed by another. I lay there fretting, and the next thing I remember is seeing blue lights flashing on the bedroom wall.

Soon I could hear fire engines too. Their sirens were blaring up and down the street.

I jumped out of bed and pulled back the blanket on the window. Derek's house was on fire! I could see bright orange flames climbing up the walls and leaping from the windows.

I was so shocked I ran over to Daddy and shook him awake, shouting, 'Wake up, Daddy! Derek's house is on fire. Do something! Help them!'

He woke up and spat, 'Get back into bed and shut your mouth, you little bitch.' I couldn't believe how cold and uncaring he was. Even though I was only twelve-years-old, I could tell a terrible tragedy was unfolding, but my daddy simply reacted with anger.

I ran downstairs, frantic, and found Mammy and Peter outside. Lots of neighbours and all the men who lived around us were out trying to do something to help, but Mammy told me firmly to stay indoors. I went back inside, feeling terrified and upset. Margaret was a very good friend of mine, but I knew the whole family well. There were eleven kids, and nearly all of them were the same age as the kids in my family, so each Murphy child had a friend in the family. We'd played on the street together for years, and we understood each other, because we all came from a big family.

I couldn't bear the thought of them getting hurt.

After what felt like hours, Mammy came back in and told me everyone was safe, and I finally fell asleep, thanking God with all my heart for saving my friends.

Margaret was a year older than me and had started at the Technical College in Dun Laoghaire, where I would go in a few months' time. She told me everything I needed to know. They gave you free books, and the uniform was cheap, and I knew she would look out for me once I started in September. I was looking forward to it.

The next morning, Mammy told me not to go to school, and I heard arguing upstairs while I was made to stay downstairs. After a while I made out what the arguing was all about: something awful had happened and I had to be told, because if my Mammy didn't tell me I would find out as soon as I left the house.

I ran upstairs and demanded to know what was going on. Mammy just looked at me blankly, and told me straight away that the whole family had died in the fire, except Louise, Collie and Anthony.

I stood rooted to the spot in horror as the details spilled out. Louise was seriously ill in hospital. She had lain herself over Collie and Anthony, who were hiding under the bed, and saved their lives.

It didn't sound real. A picture of my dead baby floated around in my head. I could see my friend Margaret too, laughing and joking and looking all smart in her new school skirt and jumper. Now she was dead and gone, just like my baby, the baby I thought about in the dark at night but was never allowed to talk about.

Mammy kept me at home in the week running up to the funeral.

I cried all the time, when I was on my own, and didn't know how to cope with so many deaths all at once. Mammy and Daddy never said one word to comfort me and, to make matters worse, Mother Dorothy kept sending my schoolfriends to the door with messages demanding I return to school and threats that she would beat me with the cane for being absent.

Mammy told them to tell her I was far too upset to attend school, but Mother Dorothy sent them back with another message: if I wasn't at the funeral to sing in the school choir she would give me a hundred lashes.

I shuddered. I knew the choir box was upstairs in the church, and that would mean looking down on all those coffins.

The thought of all that grief and sorrow made me stiff with fear, but when the day of the funeral came I felt drawn to the church. I had to pay my last respects, and I raced in and pushed myself through the crowds at the last minute.

As I arrived I heard the pitiful strains of 'Suffer Little Children'. The coffins were being brought in now.

When I saw the small white coffin at the back, I knew it was for the baby, and I started to gasp for breath. It was like I had an invisible hand over my mouth and was being suffocated. I wanted to be sick.

I tore out of the church in a panic, carrying Michael with me. He was three-years-old, and Mammy had made me bring him. I could hear people tutting, saying how badly I was behaving. They were trying to get in, and I was forcing my way out. But I had to leave. I listened to the service from outside, where loudspeakers had been put up around the church, then staggered home in a daze, wondering why life had to be so very cruel, and what would be the next horrible thing to happen.

The next day at school, Mother Dorothy looked at me with icy eyes. 'You are a disgrace,' she told me. 'You are a terrible sinner, child. It is typical of you! You could not even pay your last respects to that family! Be sure your sins will find you out!'

She beat me mercilessly with the cane for not singing in the choir, just as she had threatened. Even when I protested that I was distraught about losing all my friends like that, she carried on beating me.

'You're lying,' she bellowed, froth foaming from her lips. 'Another child in this school saw a lot more than you did on the night, and she managed to get herself into school.'

I bit my lip, but not because I was afraid. I was seething with anger. I remembered the time Mother Dorothy had hauled my lovely friend Margaret up to the front of the class and ridiculed her for not having brushed her hair. When Margaret said her Mammy had brushed her hair that very morning, Mother Dorothy laughed and mocked. 'How old are you? Nearly thirteen? What a big baby you are having Mammy brush your hair!'

I was so furious I wanted to slap Mother Dorothy's face. How dare she humiliate Margaret like that? She had such a short life, and Mother Dorothy caused her untold misery, just like she had me. I would never let her destroy me.

It took me a very long time to get over the fire, and bedtimes became even more frightening. A rumour went round the town that the fire had started when one of the kids dropped a cigarette down the back of the settee, and I'd lie in bed at night imagining Mammy dropping one of hers when she was drunk.

I told Mammy my fears, but she didn't listen. 'Always thinking of yourself, Cynthia,' she said. 'What about that poor family?'

She made me read out newspaper articles she'd clipped out of Daddy's papers, and told me not to be so stupid when I complained and said it upset me. 'You need to read them, Cynthia,' she said. 'You need to cry. Why don't you cry, Cynthia?'

It seemed to really bother her that I didn't cry, but I felt frozen inside. I could tell my reaction disturbed Mammy though, because she wouldn't let it drop.

I'd tell her to leave me alone, but she shoved the pictures of the little white coffins under my nose and taunted me time and time again. I couldn't cry. I was paralysed with grief, but Mammy said I was a heartless bitch. She said that to other people too, but I knew it wasn't true. If anyone came to the house, she forced me to read out the clippings, and when I didn't cry she scoffed, 'Here, see. Didn't I tell you she was a heartless bitch?' She never let it drop, ever.

Mammy had told me to 'shut and stop complainin'' so many times that I had become quite good at stopping myself from crying. Another thought struck me one day, and it frightened me. If I started to cry, how would I stop? Would I cry for my baby too? I didn't want to do that, it was too hard, and it would cause too many arguments.

Finally, one time when Mammy shoved those photos under my nose and ordered me to cry, something snapped. I flew into a wild rage, smashing cups in the sink, throwing shoes at the walls and knocking down pictures.

'There now – is this what you want?' I screeched. 'You wanted me to react – are you happy now?' But still I didn't cry.

Mammy just laughed at me, and then she took great delight in telling any visitors to our house that I had gone crazy and smashed it up, just because she asked why I didn't cry for that poor family.

One night, when I was lying in bed unable to sleep, she crept upstairs with a matchbox containing a horsefly.

She knew I was scared of those straggly-legged insects, and she dropped it on top of me, laughing hysterically and saying, 'Why don't you cry, Cynthia? Why don't you cry!'

Bedtime had always been terrifying, but Mammy's behaviour added a frightening new dimension. Daddy was still hurting me in bed as much as ever, and I was still being dragged to that awful building.

It had become a never-ending torture I just had to survive it as best I could. Mammy's violent friend, the 'thug' still attacked me regularly too.

Now, Mammy's erratic behavior was turning me into a

complete nervous wreck. I had never known what to expect from her, but now she was getting even more unpredictable, as if she was losing her mind completely.

I was petrified of her killing herself, or killing all of us in our beds. I feared we would die in a fire, just like the family down the road. When my head hit the pillow, I never relaxed. I felt tense, and I trembled all the time, always anticipating the worst.

I spent the summer escaping to the youth club with my friends whenever I could, drinking cider and trying to forget my worries, but it never worked.

I never felt happy, not really. Even when I was laughing and joking, I felt numb inside. My heart never fluttered with joy, and I wasn't comfortable joining in when my mates started talking about pop stars they fancied and crushes they had on local boys. I didn't want to know about boys, but I did want to grow up fast, just so I could get away from Mammy and Daddy and leave all the bad things behind.

Leaving primary school and going to the Tech would be a step in the right direction. I'd dreamed of the day I would be old enough to finally walk away from Mother Dorothy, and when it came I whooped with sheer delight and relief. I never wanted to see that wicked old bag again as long as I lived. I hated her with a passion.

I was nearly thirteen now, and getting bigger and stronger. I was moving on, and life was going to get better – wasn't it?

One day, I vowed, I would get my revenge on all the people who had hurt me.

All those men would pay for what they did to me, and I would make Mammy pay for what she did to my baby, too.

Chapter 17

Nightmares and Dreams

When I joined the Tech as a determined and rebellious thirteen-year-old, my teacher told me I was intelligent and could become anything I wanted, if only I could focus on my work.

The problem was, I couldn't focus on anything except the enduring horrors of the abuse I was suffering at home and in the awful building I was still being taken to.

My brain felt permanently fogged. However much I wanted to learn and make something of my life, every day felt like a huge emotional struggle. Try as I might, I simply couldn't put all the bad things that happened away in a box in my head and pretend they didn't exist. The abuse was continuing, and by the time I was fourteen I realized I was pregnant again.

I recognized the symptoms from when I had Noleen, and I left school as soon as was legally possible. I didn't want to have to deal with questions about my changing shape, I just wanted to hide away. I didn't tell my friends about the pregnancy. I had been brought up to keep secrets, and I was still very much under my mother's control, so I said nothing.

While they spent their leisure time lazing around the beaches and going to discos Mammy, or Ma as I'd started calling her, started locking me in the house. She hid my shoes, threw my clothes in the bin and refused to give me any money.

I felt very mixed up. I stole her alcohol whenever I could and crashed out in bed, too tired to argue or care. I had no energy, and nothing to get up for. Many days just passed in a blur of boredom, misery and fear.

I gave birth for the second time in June 1976. This time my baby was stillborn. He was an incredibly tiny little boy with transparent skin, and I can only assume he was extremely premature. I was flooded with a feeling of enormous relief when he didn't breathe. Ma couldn't harm him. I couldn't love him and lose him. The decision was made, and he was already gone.

Afterwards, for the first time in a long time, I remembered Noleen very clearly. My heart ached for her, but I felt new emotions too: bitter hatred and anger towards Mammy. I no longer cared what she said or did to me, and I rebelled more than ever, smashing the house up and refusing to help with the chores.

When she hid my clothes, I'd wear anything I could lay my hands on, just to escape. My friends were fantastic and always accepted me, whatever state I turned up in. They were the ones who took me to hospital when I threw myself on to the jagged rocks in the sea one day, not caring whether I lived or died and, again, a week later, when I deliberately rode a Chopper with broken brakes down a steep hill and into a couple of parked cars. After both incidents, I was cut to ribbons and bruised black and blue, yet my parents never said a word. Granny told me the devil was trying to ruin my life and I would burn in hell. Suicide is a sin in the Catholic Church, and that's all she cared about.

Mammy's response to my behaviour was to pack me off to live with Esther in Wales when I was fifteen. My friends cried when they waved me off at the ferry at Dun Laoghaire, and tears streamed down my face. I stood on the deck holding a carrier bag with a few clothes in it, feeling utterly alone. I knew I would miss them so much. We had had such fun singing songs and mucking about together, and they had been my only source of happiness. I was devastated at leaving my four younger siblings too. I'd been like a mammy to them all, and I hated being apart from them, but as usual I couldn't argue with my mother. She ruled with a rod of iron.

Esther's house was lovely, and she made a huge effort to welcome me at first, but I struggled to settle in. I missed my friends too much, and the Welsh girls I met were so different to me. They had different tastes in fashion and music, and they didn't drink and smoke like I did at home.

I upset Esther by borrowing shoes and clothes from her neighbours' daughters, like I did with my friends back home, but it wasn't the done thing in her neighbourhood. We fell out, and after just six weeks I begged Mammy to let me go home. I started playing loud music and staying out late at night to make sure Esther would be glad to get rid of me, and eventually I got my way.

It probably sounds insane that I wanted to go back home, but I didn't see it as returning to 4 White's Villas. I saw it as returning to my friends and my siblings and everything that was familiar to me in Dalkey. The abuse had stopped after my second pregnancy. I assume, now, that I simply became too old to be a victim of child abuse, but I didn't work that out then. I was just relieved that that part of my life was over. Looking back, I think I was so traumatized that some sort of self-defence mechanism kicked in, making me shut out the memories so I didn't have to keep reliving the horrors of my past.

The sleeping arrangements had changed when I got back home. My nine-year-old brother was in the back bedroom. Little Theresa, who was five and like a sister to me, was in the double bed in the front room with my parents, and my other brother, also five, had the single bed in the same room, which I shared.

Almost as soon as I'd got back home, I noticed Mammy using Daddy as a threat to get Theresa into bed at night: 'If you're not in bed when Daddy gets home, he'll get angry and beat me,' she said.

Her words made me shudder, but I wasn't sure why.

One night, I heard my sister whimpering very quietly in

the dark. Next she was sobbing, and I could hear Daddy shuf-fling in the bed.

I lay awake, too scared to sleep. Surely Daddy wouldn't hurt her? My own abuse was pushed so far to the back of mind I didn't think about how he had abused me in the past. I didn't want to remember. I was still a child inside, and a severely traumatized one at that. I didn't have a clue how to handle the situation.

When it happened again the next night, I called out. 'Daddy, are you talking in your sleep? I think you're frightening Theresa.'

He was drunk and ignored me, so I crept downstairs and told Mammy that Daddy was scaring Theresa. Even at that age, and despite my rebellious episodes, I was still terrified of both my parents.

'He's just rolling around drunk,' said Mammy casually. The words nearly killed me, because all of a sudden I remembered when she had said that to me. I erupted with anger. 'Go up and get that filthy bastard off my sister or I will smash this house up.' Mammy laughed and said I was crazy. The next night she sent me to sleep in the back bedroom, and I obeyed. Being in that house made me feel like a helpless child again.

I drank to forget whenever I could, but one night Theresa smiled at me with her beautiful brown eyes and I felt an enor-mous pang of guilt. How could I stand by and let her be harmed?

I now drank whatever I could get my hands on. For a while

I even downed bottles of cough mixture, just to block out my past and what was happening now. I drank cider regularly with my friends at the youth club, too, and it was there that I met the man who became my first husband, when I was fifteen and drunk.

The first time I took him home, Mammy amazed me by welcoming him with open arms, and she seemed thrilled when he eventually proposed. I agreed to marry him, mainly because I desperately wanted to get out of 4 White's Villas.

Around this time, I had dreadful flashbacks of Noleen dying. I saw blood on her face and a knitting needle in a hand. I knew something awful had happened in my childhood, but I was terrified of confronting my memories, and I just didn't analyse them. I hoped moving out might help me leave the terrors of the past behind.

I was nineteen and pregnant again when I got married. Daddy came with me in the wedding car. I wanted to feel lovely sitting there in my flowing white gown, but when I looked at Daddy's dirty fingernails and smelled the stale smoke on his breath, I just felt sick. I knew he was part of the horror of my childhood, but I didn't dare think too deeply about it, even when the familiar feelings of pregnancy tormented me with dark and distant memories. They were just too horrible to explore.

I'd been elated when the doctor confirmed I was expecting, and I told myself I would cherish this baby and surround it with so much love you wouldn't believe it. That was my plan.

I was moving on to a happy new phase in my life, or so I hoped.

I gave birth in the summer. When my waters broke, it stirred terrible black thoughts in my head, but again I tried to block them out. Ma had offered to be with me for the birth, but I didn't want her anywhere near me. She still scared me, even now I was a married woman. She offered to knit a jacket for the new baby, despite the fact she hadn't done any knitting for many years.

Her behaviour baffled me at the time, because she was being uncharacteristically helpful, but I know now she was trying to put the past behind her too, to save her own neck. If only it were that easy.

It was a difficult birth, and my baby son was placed in an incubator. 'Mammy loves you,' I whispered, holding his tiny hand in mine. I felt an overwhelming surge of love for him. It was so powerful it took my breath away. I knew in that instant that I had never loved anyone as much as I loved that little boy. 'I will always love you,' I told him. 'I will never let anyone take you away from me.' I loved being a mum and tried to make a success of my new start, but I couldn't escape my memories and soon found myself having nightmares about my younger siblings left at home. Many times I got up and raced miles through the streets in the dark, banging on Mammy's door to check they were safe. Each time, she shooed me away nastily and said I was crazy.

One day, my little sister Theresa had volunteered to babysit for me and didn't turn up, which was very unusual. I knew something was wrong, and I got it out of her that Martin, now sixteen, had tried to gas himself in the kitchen at 4 White's Villas.

I dashed to the hospital, to learn that this had been no cry for help: he had been very lucky to survive. Ma arrived soon afterwards, marching manically up the corridor searching for news.

'Oh look at the nosy cow,' she crowed. 'She *would* have to get her big nose in, wouldn't she!'

'You don't know if your son is dead or alive, but you can always take a moment to attack me,' I scowled back. 'You need to look after him better.' After this, I invited Martin to my flat often, but it wasn't much of an escape for him, as I had my own problems. My husband and I weren't getting on, and we split up when our son was a young boy.

Sadly, for reasons I can't discuss, I missed out on many years of my son's childhood. I tried everything in my power not to lose a single day with him, but all I can say is that fate was unbelievably cruel to me. The pain of not seeing my son was unbearable, and I felt it every day. For a long time it hurt me just to breathe.

When we ended the marriage, I found myself homeless too, because in Ireland there was then no State housing for women who left their husbands and the family home. Friends helped me out, and I even moved to England for a while, just so I could stay in a homeless hostel and receive benefits. It didn't work out, and one night I was forced to return to 4 White's Villas. I simply had nowhere else to go.

Michael and Theresa were fifteen-years-old by then, and both were bright and beautiful people. I loved spending time with them again, but something made me shudder when I saw how they slipped silently out of the room when my daddy walked in. He seemed to make their brightness fade, as if he cast a black shadow over them. It was unnerving.

I couldn't bring myself to sleep upstairs in the house that first night. I told myself it was because the beds were filthy, just like they always were, and because that stinking toilet bucket was still on the floor, after all those years. The truth was I didn't want to relive my childhood. How could I even begin to cope if I allowed myself to remember so many terrible things?

I slept downstairs and, the next morning, before anyone else was awake, I slipped out and caught a ferry back to England. I found myself digs in Worksop, where I'd stayed before and had friends, but I wasn't living. I was barely functioning.

After a while, I moved to a block of flats, and there I met Tony. I was desperate for love, and I welcomed his attention whenever he called in for a chat and a cup of tea. He kissed me one day, and a flicker of life sparked inside me.

I put my arms round him and enjoyed his hugs.

Tony made me feel human and lovable for the first time in many years. When we started sleeping together a few months later, he would hold me all night long, while I cried on his shoulder for my son.

We'd been together several months when I realized I was pregnant. I'd been on the Pill for years now, and I was horrified when the doctor confirmed my suspicions. My relationship with Tony was far from perfect. I started behaving unreasonably, resenting him for making me pregnant, and our relationship quickly started to unravel. By the time I gave birth, in the summer of 1987, Tony and I had separated. All I wanted to do was focus on my new baby boy. This time, I vowed that nothing would go wrong. I ached to be a mother to this child, and was determined nothing would ruin things.

I fell in love with Christopher the moment he was born. He was beautiful, and I hugged him to my chest and started to cry. He reminded me of another little baby, but I couldn't remember which one. I lay there for hours, trying to work it out, but it didn't come to me. Perhaps I wouldn't let it.

Christopher was a month old when I bumped into Simon in the street while I was out shopping for nappies. I'd known him for a while through my friends in Worksop, and when he saw me alone with the new baby he offered to come round and help me out.

I'd moved into a council house, which my friends had decorated while I was in hospital, and for the first time in my life I had a home I felt proud of. I was besotted with Christopher, and when I saw Simon lift him tenderly out of his cot, something in me stirred. He looked like a daddy – a proper daddy.

Christopher gurgled, and Simon and I exchanged smiling glances.

We spent many more happy hours together after that. Simon never shouted or swore. He didn't criticize me or bully me or run me down. Instead, he paid me compliments, made me laugh, he held me tight and listened. Before long, I was besotted with him too. When we made love, it was so tender and loving that I felt completely safe for the first time in my life.

I started to sleep more soundly than I ever had, and Simon told me many times, 'I'm here for you. I'll never let you down.' I joked to my friends that he was like someone you read about in a girls' magazine. He was my perfect man in every way, and he became a perfect father to Christopher. I was happier and more settled than I'd ever been.

One dark night in 1990, I woke up screaming from a nightmare. It started out as the same nightmare I'd had the night before, and the night before that. I was a small child sleeping in the single bed in the front room at 4 White's Villas. It was dark and cold, and someone got into bed with me and put their arms around me, but it didn't make me feel safe and warm. I felt scared.

On previous nights, that's where the dream had ended. But this time, when the person hugged me, I saw who it was. It was my father, and I was trembling and shaking. He terrified me, and I sat up in bed, struck with panic.

'It's all right,' Simon whispered. 'Don't cry! It's just a nightmare. You'll be all right in the morning, you'll see.' I lay awake for hours, Simon's arms wrapped round me, and when dawn broke I sat up in bed feeling nauseous. I felt the blood drain from my face, and my legs went weak. I ran to the toilet and vomited.

The same thing happened without warning many more times over the next year. I knew I wasn't pregnant, as I'd chosen to be sterilized after Christopher's birth. But before my period each month, my stomach swelled up, I was moody and irritable and my breasts were sore. After each nightmare I wanted to vomit, and I couldn't face wearing bright colours. I wanted to dress only in black. It felt like I was in mourning, but I didn't know who had died.

I was almost thirty-years-old by then, and I was determined I wasn't going to lose the new life I had. Simon and Christopher meant everything to me. I wasn't going mad, was I? I went to my doctor and asked for help. 'I think I have some issues to deal with,' I said, not knowing what else to say. 'I think I need to talk to a professional.' Within weeks, I saw a psychiatrist, who told me almost immediately he had good news. 'You aren't mad,' he said. 'I think you just have some unresolved problems from your childhood.' I was referred to Maureen, a community psychiatric nurse, who was to give me therapy to help me solve the issues.

Around the same time, Theresa asked if she could come and stay for a while, and Simon and I readily agreed. She was almost twenty now, and we got on brilliantly. Not only that, but she could help out with Christopher while I went to my therapy sessions. It was perfect.

Maureen didn't judge, she just listened. I was starting to feel better. Theresa and I went on bike rides, sang Diana Ross songs into our hairbrushes together like teenagers and took Christopher to feed the ducks.

One morning in November 1991, we were standing in my bedroom by an open window. It was a crisp winter's day, and the view of the open countryside with the dawn mist lifting off the fields was breathtaking. Theresa started talking to me. I didn't hear her words at first, but as I turned to face her, the beautiful views in my brain suddenly turned to black.

'Daddy sexually abused me as a child. Mammy told me last time I visited.' My stomach turned over. 'How can you be sure?' I heard myself saying. 'Do you remember?' Theresa said she had memories of Daddy doing something to her in bed at night. She remembered crying a lot, and feeling a lot of pain. The memories made her feel suicidal, and she confided she had tried to take her own life several times.

As she spoke, I heard a muffled sort of cry, a cry I'd heard before. My mind started to spin, and I thought I was going to pass out. I sat on the bed to steady myself. 'Do you really believe you were abused, Theresa?' I asked.

She nodded, looking embarrassed. I looked at her sad brown eyes and I saw the beautiful little girl I played mammy to all those years ago. 'I will support you. I will do whatever it takes,' I told her, though my mind was in turmoil.

Deep down, I knew those nightmares I had about Daddy meant he had touched me too, in a way he shouldn't have.

That's why I had asked for therapy. It all clicked into place. I knew what it meant, and I knew I had to face it.

I trusted Maureen implicitly, and I told her everything Theresa had said, adding that in my nightmares I was sure it was my father abusing me. It felt like the earth was shifting beneath my feet, and dark doors were opening in my mind. Coping with daily life became a struggle. Without Simon's support, I would not have got through each day.

I spent much of that year in a pit of depression. Every memory that came back broke my heart. I remembered the neglect, the filth and the poverty. I could feel the headlice and the fleas and the beatings, and I recalled the drunken fights and violent arguments.

My parents were alcoholics, and they abused and neglected me.

I had never acknowledged how dysfunctional they were. As the truth dawned, I became a nervous wreck. I shouted at Simon and snapped at Christopher. I wished I could turn back time and throw all my memories back into that black box, locked away for ever in the back of my mind. But it was too late for that.

One morning, I felt a powerful urge to clean the house. Everybody was out, and I walked into Christopher's bedroom to tidy his toys off the floor. I looked at his bed and, in a daze, lay down on it. The second I touched the duvet, my body seemed to shrink. I felt like a little girl again, and suddenly my body started to jerk up and down. My mind was travelling back down dark corridors, back through the years. When it stopped travelling, I was in the single bed at home in Dalkey. Daddy was in the bed with me, and I started crying.

'No, Daddy, no! Please, Daddy, no!' I cried out. My mind went oil black as the pain ripped through me. I thought I was going to split in two.

Moments later, I was back in Christopher's room, looking at his blue-striped duvet cover and the picture of Spiderman on the wall. I didn't move for hours. I just lay there sobbing.

I told Simon that night that my father had raped me as a young girl.

'I will look after you,' he told me tenderly, but I could see he was in shock too. And I was inconsolable.

I tried to carry on living as normal a life as possible, for Christopher's sake. He had started school, and I joined a secretarial college, where I worked as hard on my studies as I did on trying to appear happy and normal like everybody else.

One Sunday night, in April 1993, I was lying in bed when a series of vivid memories made my spine stiffen. They came from nowhere, and I felt like I'd been electrocuted.

'Oh my God, I was pregnant as a child!' I called out.

Bizarre images blazed around my head. I saw sanitary towels and a sanitary belt, vitamins and raw eggs and liver. I tasted salt water in my mouth.

I had to tell Maureen. I had already confided to her that my father had actually raped me, but it was even harder telling her I was pregnant as a child.

I said it quietly, eyeing her carefully to judge her reaction.

'I know,' she said, nodding gently.

'How can you know?' I gasped.

'I've been waiting for you to tell me, Cynthia.' I was astonished. I sat rooted to the spot as Maureen explained how many of the other memories I'd shared, plus the vomiting and bloating I experienced around my periods, pointed to me suffering a pregnancy in childhood. She had had to wait for me to mention it first, because that was the way therapy worked. Everything had to come from me.

I shared all this news with Simon, but felt guilty burdening him. He didn't doubt me or judge me, and I loved him more for that, if it were possible.

'I'll stand by you, come what may,' he said.

I needed every ounce of his love and compassion, especially when I started having vivid recollections of the night Noleen died and the many sickening ways in which my father abused me.

Flashbacks came when I was reading to Christopher or cooking the dinner. I started staying downstairs at night, huddled by the dying embers of the coal fire.

I chain-smoked, and my body shook from head to toe as I relived one memory after another. I often stayed there until dawn, too scared to get into bed.

'I want to move away and make a fresh start,' I told Simon one day.

I desperately hoped that I could somehow learn to live with my memories and life would return to some sort of normality.

Simon agreed to give it a try. Our relationship was being tested, and we both welcomed the chance to make it better.

We moved to Scarborough in September 1993, and Simon found a new job as a taxi driver.

The first few months went well, but one night I was alone in the house when I suddenly felt like I had a spider inside my stomach. It was climbing slowly up towards my mouth and was about to spill out and make me scream.

I thought I was going mad. I put on some old Irish music and drank some vodka to dull the fright and wash the spider away.

As the sharp liquid slid down my throat, my memories started crowding round my head.

They were like ghosts and devils, haunting me and taunting me. I couldn't shake them off. I saw Daddy's dirty finger-nails clawing me. And I saw Ma stabbing my baby in the face.

'No!' I screamed at the shadows. 'No!'

When Simon came in, I was drunk and hysterical. 'I have to stop living this lie,' I sobbed. 'I did have a baby, and I'm going to find that baby!'

'Go to the police then,' he said tenderly. 'What else can you do?'

I laughed. 'And tell them what? They'll think I'm mental. They'll lock me up.'

'If you are telling the truth, they won't,' Simon said calmly.

I knew he was right, but in the cold light of day I was too frightened to call the police.

My mother had always told me I was crazy and a liar. I knew the police might say the same thing.

Christmas was coming, and I welcomed the distraction. Christopher had put up with a lot of upheaval, and I vowed to make it up to him.

I wanted to spend Christmas Day laughing and playing with him, but as soon as I smelled the turkey cooking I wanted to vomit.

I ran to the bathroom, feeling infected with turkey. It was everywhere, suffocating and poisoning me. I scrubbed my hands, then my whole body, and I vomited violently. Apologizing to Christopher, I wrapped myself up on the sofa, thinking I must have a virus.

'It's OK, Mum,' he said, and as he spoke a bulb flashed in my mind.

Daddy was banging on the floor. I was carrying up his turkey dinner. And now he was hauling me across his lap and pulling down my pants.

The same images flashed before me. I saw those Christmas days. The decorations and the presents were slightly different in each memory, but every time I ended up crying in pain in Daddy's bed.

'The bastard! A voice screamed inside my head. I looked at Christopher unwrapping his presents by the tree. Each time he laughed with joy, my heart twanged.

How could parents harm their own child? Had my father's childhood in the orphanage damaged him so much that he didn't know his behaviour was so wrong?

I agonized for months and months about phoning the police. One Sunday morning in April 1994, Simon, Christopher and I went for a drive to the beach.

The sun was shining, and Christopher was playing contentedly with a toy on the back seat when I glimpsed myself as an eight-year-old girl, in bed with Daddy. I was telling him he hurt me, and I was crying and whimpering and begging him to stop.

My mind clicked back to Christopher. I pictured our play fights on the living-room carpet. We rolled around and tickled each other, but whenever Christopher said, 'Stop, Mum! That hurts!' I stopped immediately and gave him a cuddle to say sorry.

My face was bathed in sunlight, and I felt warm tears trickle down my cheeks.

Whatever had happened in his past, my father couldn't say he didn't know it was wrong to hurt me. The second I told him he was hurting me and I wanted him to stop, he should have stopped.

Instead he tied my arms with a belt to stop me struggling free.

The full force of his evil hit me, right there in the car. You stupid cow, I told myself. Of course he knew it was wrong. He's a wicked child-abuser. There can be no excuse.

What if he's still abusing other children? You cannot sit back and do nothing.

'Are you OK?' Simon asked, noticing my tears.

'Yes,' I replied. 'The minute I get back home, I'm ringing the police.'

I spent many hours giving a statement to North Yorkshire Police about the sexual abuse I suffered as a child.

The interviews were unbearably upsetting, but liberating too. I had taken the first step towards seeing my parents locked up in jail, where they belonged.

When I got home, deep fear kicked in. I was dealing with sick paedophiles. My mother was a murderer. What would happen next?

One night, Simon came home from work, got down on one knee and asked me to marry him.

He had asked me a million times before, but I had always refused.

I loved him to bits, but the timing had never been right. There was always a trauma going on, and I always put him off, afraid that marriage might change our wonderful relationship.

'Yes, let's get married,' I whispered back. 'I'm ready now.'

Simon looked surprised and delighted.

'I love you,' I told him, then found myself adding, 'And I want you to legally adopt Christopher.'

I explained to Simon I'd had dark thoughts during my lonely nights in bed when he was out working. I was terrified that when my statement hit the Irish Police, something terrible could happen to me.

'If I die, I want you to be Christopher's next of kin. I do not want my parents to have any claim on him, ever.'

He kissed me tenderly. 'I love you and I want to look after you and Christopher for ever,' he told me.

We had a simple wedding in August 1994, and I cried tears of joy.

I knew Simon truly loved me, and would do anything for me.

Within weeks of our marriage, the police talked to my family in Ireland.

I was working full-time by then, for a building society in Scarborough, running a small department.

Despite an appalling attendance record at college, I'd come out with outstanding grades and was determined to carve out a good career for myself. I didn't want to give my parents the satisfaction of stealing my education as well as everything else.

Besides, my job gave me a focus when I woke up with a black cloud of depression over my head. With Christopher at school, I needed to keep busy while I waited for news from the police in Ireland.

I was doing a pretty good job until 10 March 1995, when Esther phoned unexpectedly. I hadn't heard from her for a while, and I asked if she had any news.

There was a long silence on the end of the phone.

'You don't know, do you, Cynthia?' she said finally.

'What are you talking about, Esther?'

'Wait,' she said. 'I'll go to the phone in the other room.'

As soon as I heard her breathe again, I asked, 'Who has died, Esther?'

As I said the words, I was sure it was our mother. All those suicide threats over the years flashed before me. She was a coward, and it was the only way she could escape the police closing in on her. It had to be her.

But Esther said another name. She said the name Martin. My little brother, Martin.

I went dizzy. I repeated his name time and time again, gasping for air and shaking my head.

'How, Esther? When?'

Martin had killed himself in our family home, banging a nail into the door in the living room, the one leading to the hallway that backed on to the bedrooms, and hanging himself. He was twenty-seven-years old.

I sobbed and shook.

I found out later, that he had been terrified and ashamed of it coming out that he had been sexually abused by my father.

He had died three months previously, but nobody had told me because my father didn't want me at the funeral.

I hung up the phone and lit a cigarette, even though at that point I hadn't smoked for years.

I watched the smoke swirl in the air as I remembered Martin sitting by my desk in his buggy, looking at me longingly with his big bright eyes.

I shifted on the sofa. I recalled how Martin used to try and sleep fully clothed on the sofa in the sitting room sometimes. Now it was clear to me that it must have been in order to avoid the beds upstairs at 4 White's Villas.

Back then, my head was fogged with pills and drink and pain and confusion. I didn't know how tortured our lives were, or how wrong the abuse was.

But I was a grown-up woman now, and my mind was clear. I knew how terribly wrong it was. I knew it wasn't normal; and I knew we didn't deserve it.

My parents were sick paedophiles, that was the shocking truth.

When Simon got home, I sobbed in his arms, telling him how it was all my fault Martin had died.

I remembered his suicide attempt when he was sixteen. How could I have put him through all this torment?

I blamed myself every single day. I gave up my job because I couldn't cope. I needed all my strength to survive, and to carry on my fight. I was not going to let Martin die in vain.

The inquest had taken place without my knowledge, and I found out later that my father told the coroner he believed Martin had killed himself because he was a drug addict and alcoholic.

I also discovered that Martin had warned my mother exactly when, where and why he was going to kill himself.

She should have got help for Martin, but she didn't because then the real reason he was suicidal would have come out.

Instead, she threatened that, if he killed himself, she would not attend his funeral, and she kept her threat and stayed away when he was buried.

I was incensed. Who did she think she was? Did she think she had the right to decide who lived and died, and who knew about the death?

I screamed in rage. This had to stop.

North Yorkshire police were focusing their investigation on the sexual abuse I suffered at home as a child. Ensuring the safety of other children my father had contact with was, of course, their top priority.

But I decided it was time to speed things up. It was twenty-two years since Noleen had died, and I had waited long enough to punish my mother for her crime. I wanted a murder investigation too.

It was very late one night in April 1995 when I finally found the courage to call Dun Laoghaire police station.

Simon and Christopher were sleeping, and the only sound I could hear was my own blood gushing though my brain. It sounded like a waterfall. I took a deep breath and spoke slowly.

'Do you remember the baby that was found dead in Lee's Lane in the 1970s?' I said to the officer on duty. 'Well, I am the mother of that baby.'

It was a giant step and, just as I'd hoped, things did indeed move quickly after that, at least to begin with.

The police dug out Noleen's unsolved murder file from 1973.

They took me back to Lee's Lane to point to the spot where I had left her in the bag, and a few months later my parents were arrested and brought in for questioning.

It was a massive breakthrough, and I was jangling with nerves as I waited at the police station, knowing my parents were under the same roof, finally facing their demons.

The hours dragged by as their questioning went on. I had agreed to confront them if they didn't confess.

At lunchtime, I asked if I could visit Noleen's grave.

I'd been given the number of the plot and had burned it into my memory, afraid it might be snatched away again. At last I felt the time was right to pay my respects.

The police took me to Glasnevin cemetery. Even though Noleen was a murder victim, she had been buried in a cardboard box in the communal 'Little Angels' plot with nineteen other babies.

While the officers searched for the grave, I was drawn to a bare plot that was nothing more than a mound of rough earth.

'This is it,' I said instinctively, and the number confirmed I was right. A feeling of strength washed over me as I stared at the barren ground.

I had found her after all these years.

I crouched down, laid a small bunch of flowers on the earth, and spoke quietly.

'I have loved and missed you all these years. My arms have ached to hold you. I am sorry I have taken so long. Do you forgive me? I will make it up to you. I will make them pay.'

I cried all the way back to the police station.

Neither of my parents had confessed to a single crime. It was 5 p.m., and the police had until 9 p.m. to charge or release them. I had to confront them and was shown into an interview room.

I recoiled in shock when I saw Mammy sitting at a round table, surrounded by five officers. I hadn't seen her for nine years, but time rolled back and I felt instantly scared in her presence.

'Hi, Mammy,' I said quietly, as a detective pointed to my place across the table.

Her face was hard and cold, and she looked as brazen as if she was sitting at her own kitchen table.

'Well, you said you would get us,' she replied.

'What do you mean?' an officer interjected.

'I mean she has always hated me and she is doing this to spite me,' she spat.

My body was shaking and my emotions were screaming out in confusion.

For a second I wanted to run and throw my arms around her. I wanted her to tell me she loved me and that she was sorry, but when I looked at her again she was giving me a cold, evil stare, one that shot me straight back to my childhood.

She was trying to unhinge me. She was trying to get through

to that little girl inside me, the one who was so scared of her that, even when she was holding my murdered baby in her arms, I obeyed her command to get back in the house, and slipped inside the sitting room, just because my mammy told me to.

I've often wondered how different my life and so many other lives, would have been had I had the courage to run away that night.

I wasn't a little girl any more, and I looked her in the eye.

'Would you please tell them about my baby and what you did to her?' I demanded.

'I don't know what you are talking about.'

My blood boiled, and I pointed my trembling finger at her. 'You killed my baby. You stabbed her with a knitting needle in front of me.'

Her mouth fell open, and she threw her nicotine-stained hands up to her face in horror.

'May God forgive you!' she wailed dramatically.

I exploded with frustration. 'Will you come with me to the lane where we dumped her tiny body, and tell me then you did not kill my daughter?'

'I would be too embarrassed,' she said pathetically. 'People would be looking. I'd collapse!'

'Well, I had to do it!' I bellowed. 'I had to face it. Why shouldn't you?'

She shook her head defiantly.

'Come to the grave then,' I goaded.

'No.'

'Why not? If you are so innocent, why can't you come to her grave with me? Why did you kill my baby? Why?'

'You never liked me, and you always said you would get me,' she replied.

'Is that all you can say? Why did you feed me raw eggs and liver? Why did you send me to my father's bed on Christmas Day?'

She continued to glare at me in a mocking, intimidating way, and I began to feel frightened.

An officer put his arm around me and told her to stop staring at me.

Her denials went on. She denied ever knowing I was sexually abused. 'I'd have helped her if I'd known,' she lied through her yellow teeth.

'What about that man?' I asked. 'The one you made me sing "Scarlet Ribbons" to, and then forced me into bed with?'

'That was all very innocent,' she replied, seemingly unrattled.

'Cynthia is a liar,' she went on. 'She used to steal chips off her younger brothers' and sisters' plates. She was a terrible child to raise.'

I laughed cynically. 'Is that all you have on me?'

An officer reminded her they were not here to talk about me. My mother was the one being questioned about murdering a baby.

'She tells lies,' she repeated over and over again, regardless of what we threw at her. 'She makes things up. She's mad. If there was a baby, then she must have murdered it herself in the lane.'

I left the interview room exhausted and defeated at 8.10 p.m., after more than three hours with my mother.

She was nearly sixty-two-years-old. She had been arrested, locked in a cell and then grilled for twelve hours, but she never once showed the slightest sign she might give up any one of her sordid secrets.

She was pure evil, and I was heartbroken.

I was immediately beckoned to another room. I walked up to the door and glanced through the glass.

My father was sitting inside, and I gasped in shock and stood nailed to the spot for several minutes, trying to give myself the strength to go in.

He looked shaken. His body was jangling from head to toe, like he had lost all control of himself.

I said hello as I opened the door, and he looked up at me and said, 'What's that?'

'That's your daughter,' the detective told him.

'I don't know her. Get her out of here,' my father scoffed.

'You should know me,' I said sternly. 'Because you are the one who raped me.'

He pointed to the statement on the desk in front of him and jabbed his finger at it.

He stank of stale cigarette smoke, and his fingernails were black as coal. I winced.

'I've said what I've got to say,' he said.

'Please tell the truth,' I begged desperately. I knew the clock was ticking. I had to get him to talk.

'I'm sick of her lies,' was all he could say.

I made one last, desperate attempt to find his conscience. 'Daddy, will you not just admit I was pregnant as a child? Please?'

'She's mad!' he screamed. 'Get her out! I want judge and jury on this. I want to put her to shame.'

'I've got the shame of what you did to me for the rest of my life,' I shouted. 'Please tell them the truth!'

But his eyes were dead and his mouth was set in stone.

I walked out and felt as if I was falling apart. I had expected my mother to be a cold, evil bitch, but I had hoped my father might find it in himself to tell the truth.

How wrong I was. I looked back at his trembling body and felt nothing but contempt. He was a cold, evil monster too.

At 9 p.m. they were both released without charge, but all was not lost.

There were other avenues to explore in my quest for justice, and I agreed to everything the police asked of me to keep the investigation going.

I underwent nine hours of interviews with a psychologist and a psychiatrist, who both verified my sanity and the consistency of my story.

I also had to identify Noleen from two photographs.

I could sense I was plunging deeper into hell, but I told myself to be strong. I was doing it for her.

I already knew my baby had been stabbed forty times. She weighed 5lbs 5oz and was 18.5 inches long.

The wound that killed her was in her neck, but my mother had gone on stabbing her repeatedly, even after she had died.

I opened the blue photograph folder very slowly, with shaking hands, and the second my eyes fell on my daughter's body I had to look away in horror – but it was too late.

I saw Noleen's beautiful fair hair and how perfect she had been, but I also saw how she was laid on a mortuary slab, her tiny body covered in stab marks.

One was on her chin. I remembered my mother stabbing her there, because I remember thinking she had a dimple like my father.

I slammed the folder shut and jumped out of my seat to get away from it.

'Can you identify that child as your daughter?' the policeman asked.

'Yes, that is my daughter,' I said. 'That is my daughter, Noleen.'

I had never named her before that day, but I'd recently asked my good friend Diane to help me choose one.

Diane had been my long-suffering friend for seven years and had been a rock. Noleen was her middle name, and when she suggested it I thought it was perfect.

As incredible as it may seem, it took twelve long years from that point on for Noleen's name to be formally recognized, and for the cause of her death to be publicly recorded at her inquest.

The police didn't exhume Noleen's body, because of the passage of time and the fact she was in a communal grave, so there was no chance of linking me to her though DNA evidence. My parents were never prosecuted, because of lack of evidence, and when I eventually plucked up the courage to report the abuse I'd suffered at the hands of all those other men at the building, they were never prosecuted either. Lack of evidence was cited in each case.

With each setback, I refused to give up hope of finding justice for Noleen. Simon supported me every step of the way, telling me I had to follow my heart.

We held a memorial service for Noleen in April 1996, and Theresa stood with me as I laid a bunch of pink and white carnations on the grave. I placed a card there, which said:

'To Noleen, cry no more. Sleep in peace. Two broken hearts have been mended.'

I hadn't seen Theresa for several years. Our shared memories of abuse had been too much to bear, and it became too painful to spend time together, but I was comforted to see how well she looked that day.

She was stunningly beautiful, with her glossy dark hair and pale skin. Somehow, she had found the strength to push forward with her life, and she had a good job, travelling the world as a nanny to a famous pop star. I was delighted for her.

I was suffering from crippling depression as my legal battle dragged on and on.

In time, the Minister for Justice said she could not help me, and the European Court of Human Rights turned me down flat.

I was struggling to sleep at night. I had frightening flash-backs of my father grabbing at me in bed, and I often woke up screaming.

Sometimes I couldn't bear to let Simon touch me. That hurt me so much. I loved my husband dearly, and it felt like my parents even had the power to damage my marriage, which infuriated me and fuelled my fight.

My luck finally changed in 2000, when I was introduced to Gerry Dunne, a Dublin solicitor who knew of my case and wanted to help. He had a top barrister, Kieron Wood, on board too, as well as Michael Forde, a senior member of counsel.

They were a godsend. It was Gerry who first suggested we could ask for Noleen's inquest to be re-opened. It had been opened and adjourned on 27 April 1973, but to formally identify Noleen could only improve my chances of prosecuting my parents. For the first time ever, I wasn't feeling my way through the legal system on my own. It would take time, but I could see light at the end of the tunnel.

I was doing the housework one morning in June 2002 when I got a text message from an old friend in Ireland:

'Did you know Michael has gone missing? I read it in the paper.'

I grabbed the phone, instantly in a panic, and called Dalkey police station for confirmation.

'Yes, Mrs Owen, he has been missing for nine days now.'

I was paralysed with shock. Was he lying dead somewhere?

I sat in bed shaking, and didn't eat, sleep or even wash for four whole days.

I lived for the phone to ring with good news, but it never did. I felt laden with guilt. I had practically raised Michael single-handed as a baby. I hadn't seen him for a while. Had I neglected him, too caught up with fighting for Noleen?

My parents were both in their seventies by this time, and living comfortably in a retirement bungalow in Sallynoggin, not far from Dalkey. It sickened me to think of them pottering happily around while Martin lay dead and Michael was missing.

My desire to punish them for their crimes was so strong it spurred me on, despite the terrible trauma Michael's disappearance brought me.

It was nearly three years before he was found. In my heart I had known my little brother had to be dead. His decomposed body was finally found at Killiney Station on 1 February 2005.

A few weeks later I spoke to Theresa for the first time in ages, and I was shocked when I heard her voice. The strong and confident woman I'd been so proud of at Noleen's memorial service sounded like a scared little girl again.

'I can't get over Michael,' she said in the thinnest of whispers. 'I heard you're still fighting. You're stronger than me, but you'll never win against those bastards.'

Her voice frightened me. 'Theresa, I am coming to Ireland tomorrow to see you,' I said.

When we met, she cried in my arms like a baby for three harrowing hours.

She told me Michael's death had triggered horrific memories of the pair of them being raped by my father, and she couldn't get them out of her head.

'I keep having flashbacks of Mammy ripping at her own arms with needles and putting her head in the gas oven, telling us she's going to kill herself,' Theresa sobbed.

'Then she's forcing us upstairs to sleep with her dirty bastard of a husband, so he could rape us instead of her.'

Hearing her sum up my own memories so bluntly was agonizing. We had shared the same pain as children, and we were still sharing it.

'I cried in desperate fear going up those stairs every night. "It's your turn, Michael," I'd sob. "No, it's your turn, Theresa." We'd fight and hit each other, even though we loved each other so much. Then that bastard would be shouting, "Get in here, now!"

'I can see him now, pissing in the bucket then pulling me into his bed and pinning me against the wall. I can still smell the shit and drink all over him.

'After he raped me, I'd scream and literally climb the walls, shouting out for help. He punched and kicked me, telling me to shut up, and if I escaped downstairs then Mammy, that wicked witch, would tell me, "Get back up those stairs. He'll beat me or rape me if you don't. Go on, if you don't want your Mammy to die!" She was never a mammy to me. You were my real mammy, not her. I love you so much.'

I rocked Theresa gently in my arms and told her I was sure we would get justice one day. I had a top legal team behind me now, she would see.

I spoke the words bravely, but inside I was shattered.

Once again, I had left Simon struggling to juggle his work with running the home and, with a heavy heart, I returned to England.

How I wish I could turn the clock back and never have let go of Theresa. Within days of my leaving, she ended her life.

Just as Martin had done ten years earlier, Theresa banged a nail into a doorframe and hanged herself. She was just thirty-three-years-old.

The grief and feeling of loss was indescribable. Theresa left a thirty-five-page suicide note addressed to me.

It contained unbearably graphic accounts of how she and Michael were sexually abused by my father, with my mother's blessing.

The heartbreaking note also held her last request. Theresa didn't want my parents to see her dead. She was terrified of them being near her, even as she lay in her coffin, and she wanted to be cremated and have her ashes scattered in the Irish sea at the pier at Dun Laoghaire, to make sure they never went near her again.

Martin had been buried in a family plot, and Theresa couldn't bear the thought that one day my parents' dead bodies would lay on top of hers. That's how much they scared her.

I lay awake most nights, watching poor Simon fall slowly to sleep. How many more times did I have to burden him with my sorrows? We had three inquests to face now: Theresa's, Michael's and Noleen's.

My mother and father stayed away from Theresa's, thank God, but I was there to hear the coroner record that she had been sexually abused in childhood. It was a bittersweet victory.

Both of my parents attended Michael's inquest in 2006. I hadn't seen them in years, since I confronted them in the police station. They looked like frightening strangers to me. I was forty-four-years-old, but they made me feel nervous and insecure, like a scared little girl again.

My mother glared menacingly at me, spitting out a stream of lies and insults.

When I found the guts to glare back, she actually shouted: 'I'll fuckin' stab her in a minute.' The woman's audacity was breathtaking.

Every fibre in my body tensed when my father took the stand. He was an old man by then, well into his seventies, and when he took off his jacket he had three dirty stains on the back of his blue sweater.

I gasped audibly. I felt so ashamed of him, and it plunged me straight back to the dreadful shame I experienced throughout my childhood, when I was scruffy and dirty and smelly like him.

I listened in horror as my parents tried to destroy Michael's character, falsely accusing him of all sorts.

When I had my turn in the stand, I made sure the coroner heard the truth: Michael had been abused as a child. He was not on drugs, and he did not have a criminal record. We never found out exactly how he died.

I walked away holding my head high and feeling empowered to face my parents again at Noleen's inquest – if they weren't in jail first.

With Gerry's help, I had called for a public inquiry into my case. It was thirty-three years since Noleen had died, and it was my last hope of having my parents convicted.

My phone rang out just before midnight on 31 August 2006. Simon watched my jaw drop as I answered the call.

'What is it?' he asked. 'What's happened?'

'It's my mother,' I said flatly. 'She died three hours ago.'

Josie Murphy had died peacefully in hospital, without pain. She was seventy-three-years-old.

I broke down sobbing, not for my mother, but for the innocent lives she had destroyed.

I had waited so many years for her face her crimes in court, and I felt robbed and cheated of that right.

As the news sank in, I realized I felt great relief too. One of my abusers was dead. Her reign of terror was finally over.

Noleen's inquest took place at the Plaza Hotel in Tallaght.

Tears soaked my cheeks as I listened to the post mortem. I was reminded that, amongst Noleen's forty stab wounds, she had eighteen on her chest and fifteen on her neck. A number were inflicted after death.

Hearing those cold facts bounce off the wallpaper in the hotel conference hall made my daughter's killing sound more callous than ever.

I thought of my evil, frenzied mother. How could any human be so cruel? And how could my father sit in that court as brazenly as he did, still scowling at me like I was a piece of dirt as he clung on to his wicked secrets, a frail pensioner?

When the verdict was finally returned I was flooded with relief. I couldn't have lived if the verdict had gone against me, and having Noleen formally named as my daughter was an incredible victory.

It was the recognition I had craved for decades, and I was vindicated, to a degree.

But I'd be a liar if I said I felt justice had been done and I could live happily ever after.

All that had been proven was what I and my abusers already knew: I had a baby in my family home when I was eleven-years-old, and my baby was stabbed to death and dumped in a laneway.

Nobody had gone to prison for Noleen's murder. My mother had died peacefully, a free woman. She had got away with murder, while Martin, Michael and Theresa served life sentences of emotional torture and died in appalling circumstances.

My father still had his freedom, despite the public humili-ation the inquest had brought him.

I clung on to the hope that I'd get the public inquiry I so desperately wanted, and I was comforted when the Minister for Justice, Michael McDowell, said he was profoundly disturbed by the facts that came out of the inquest and was going to look at my case. But, it soon became clear that I wasn't going to get my public inquiry. And there was another setback: my father was calling for a judicial review of the inquest in the High Court.

I was bemused. Why bother if he had nothing to do with Noleen's conception, birth or death, as he claimed? And where on earth was the money coming from for his substantial legal bills?

I appealed against the decision not to order a public inquiry, but in November 2008 the new Minister for Justice, Dermot Ahearn, said he was sticking by it.

I was devastated. My daughter had been brutally murdered and my life had been ruined by sexual abuse. I wanted to try and meet Mr Ahearn to discuss everything, but unfortunately, that wasn't possible. The police didn't re-open Noleen's murder file, and that meant the only ongoing legal action was my father's call for the inquest to be reviewed.

My therapist diagnosed me with prolonged post-traumatic stress disorder and I struggled through every day. Simon, as ever, was my rock. He bought me flowers, gave me hugs and tried his best to keep my spirits up. He and Christopher had been my saviours, and I owed it to them to pull myself together and get back to some sort of normality.

Christmas was coming, and I was looking forward to spending some peaceful, happy time with my family. The house was twinkling with decorations when the phone rang, on 12 December 2008. It was Gerry, bearing news of another death in the Murphy family. This time it was my father. Peter Murphy senior had died of ill health at the age of eighty-two, his bid for a judicial review still outstanding. He had tortured me to his dying day.

I broke down in tears when I told Simon and Christopher. 'He never served one day behind bars,' I sobbed. 'How can this happen?' The three of us just crumbled. I felt robbed of justice, and Simon and Christopher were seething with anger.

My faith helped me survive. I do believe in God, because I don't know how I could possibly have survived that house of horrors alone. I marvel every day at how lucky I am to have survived my childhood, while Martin, Michael and Theresa didn't.

Epilogue

My son Christopher is twenty-two now, and I am very proud to say he is a happy, loving and capable man. My other son is twenty-eight-years-old.

Simon's love keeps me going in my darkest moments. He makes me smile and laugh, and I feel so blessed. I love to walk in the countryside with my dogs, read books and sit in my garden when the sun shines.

I'm very proud to have written this book. It has helped me enormously, and I can finally rest.

I sleep at night, knowing I did everything I possibly could to tell the truth and get justice for Noleen.

Acknowledgements

Many thanks to my childhood friends from Dalkey, without whom I wonder if I would have made it through my teenage years. There are too many to mention, but a special thanks to Maria O'Gorman, Michelle Hanlon, Marie Farrell, and Sheila MacGowan, and their families. To Collie and Anthony Howard, I wish you peace wherever you are. To Catherine and Alan. To Brian O'Farrell and Kevin Harran, Dave and Bridget, Christian and Elena. To Geraldine Green, Maria Kelly Whelan and Bernice Farrell. To Maggot Hutton. To Shane Brien and Uinsionn Macdubhgaill, the two boys who found my daughter's body in April 1973, when they were only eleven years old. To my friends from the Tech in Dun Laoghaire, and to the staff at the old Technical College in Dun Laoghaire. To my friends in Worksop, Nottinghamshire. To the teachers at Newark and Sherwood Secretarial School for accepting me and for educating me and, in particular, thanks to Sue Bird. To Dr Elisabeth

Noble and Dr Saffman from the Eastfield Surgery. To Dr
Pauline Graham at Scarborough Hospital. To my legal team,
Gerry Dunne and John O'Brien, and all the staff at O'Brien
Dunne Solicitors. To Kieron Wood (BL) Michael Forde (SC)
And special thanks to the many barristers and solicitors who
looked at my case over the years in an effort to help me. To
Pol O'Murchu, Felix McEnroy, James Nugent, Mary Ellen
Ring and Paul McDermott. To Alan Shatter, TD and lawyer. To
Albert Owen MP/AS and the staff at his local office, who
treated me with respect and sensitivity, a big thank you for
sticking with me, and to your secretary at the Houses of
Parliament, Gerwyn Jones. To Colm O'Gorman and Deirdre
Fitzpatrick and the staff at OneinFour. To Barry Cummins
(RTE), Brighid McLaughlin (*Sunday Independent*) and to all the
people who supported me both in the community of Dalkey
and the surrounding areas, to those who sent me flowers,
cards, letters, and emails; a big thank you from my family and
I. To Dr Dawn Henderson. To Nona and Jodie. To the coroner
Brian Farrell, thank you for being sensitive to my loss. To the
coroner Kieran Gerathy and his secretary Ciara, thank you
for doing your job. To Fr Aquinas Duffy and David Linehan
from Missing Persons for the support you gave me when my
brother Michael was missing, and for your much needed advice
and experience. To Fiona Neary Rape Crisis Centre Ireland
and to the staff at our local Rape Crisis Centre who supported
Simon and I through what was a very difficult time. To Rachel
Murphy, my co-writer, thank you for having the patience of

a saint and for not pushing me, and most of all for understanding. To the staff at Headline Publishing, in particular Carly Cook and the staff at Hachette Ireland, and my agent Jonathan Conway. And of course to my husband Simon and my son Christopher* – what can I say? It would take a million years to describe the love and loyalty you have both shown me. You taught me how to give and receive love, and how to smile and to learn to trust. The first thing I do each morning when I wake is thank God for both of you.

Cynthia can be contacted through her solicitor at:

> Cynthia Owen
> c/o Gerry Dunne
> O'Brien Dunne Solicitors
> 6 Upper Fitzwilliam Street
> Dublin 2

* Not his real name

LETTER TO MY LEGAL TEAM

Dear Gerry, Kieron and Michael,

Many times I have tried to tell you how grateful I am for what you have done for me. So many times I have tried to write it all down but I begin to cry because words cannot describe how I feel about what you have all done.

How can I find the words to say thank you to three men who gave their time so freely, who stood by me so loyally and trusted me so completely? What do I say to three men who didn't mind walking on a journey with a damaged soul and who gave me strength and picked me up every time I fell?

God knows how many time I promised myself it was over, only to discover you had all been on the phone all evening or working late into the night, and I would tell myself that if you had that much faith in me I must have faith myself.

Gerry, you had to put up with me the most. You had family holidays and kids' sports days interrupted over and over again through the years, but you never complained. You always reassured me that I was in charge and that this was about ME, which was new to me because as a child it was always about someone else and I had no voice. You gave me back my voice, and in so doing you restored me. I am in no doubt that you saved my life.

As I look back now I see that my healing was in the journey that you three came on with me, walking with me step by step.

At long last I wasn't alone anymore. I wasn't that eleven-year-old child having just lost her baby, having witnessed the most horrific crimes imaginable with no one to turn to.

You reached back to me right down through all those years and you kept me going in a world where my siblings gave up and ended their fight to survive. Yet you were always fighting for them too, and you always had them in mind and you fought for all of us.

You helped me to see there are good people in this unjust world, people who really do care and people who want to make a difference. So thank you my guardian angels, my rescuers. You gave me back my life to live, when before I met you I was merely existing.

If you know, or suspect, that a child is being abused please speak out. Remember, whilst you can choose to ignore your suspicions or choose to rescue that child. The child doesn't have the luxury of choice. Pick up the phone and ring your local Social Services, ISPCC or NSPCC and save that child's life today. If you have been abused and suspect that the abuser is still a risk to children please consider reporting him/her.

The only way to stop child abuse is to break the silence surrounding it.

'Evil prospers when good men do nothing'
Edmund Burke

If you need support or want to talk to someone about your own experiences of child sexual abuse The Rape Crisis Centre England and Wales offers support to men and women who have experienced sexual abuse in their childhood and to victims of sexual violence and rape. Their website is
http://www.rapecrisis.org.uk/centres.php

Or contact OneinFour, a registered charity that provides support to men and women who have experienced sexual abuse and or sexual violence either as adults or children.

OneinFour Office.
 219 Bromley Road Bellingham SE6 2PG
Telephone 02086972112 www.oneinfour.org.uk

Support After Murder and Manslaughter
SAMM
SAMM National
L+DRC, Tally Ho!
Pershore Road
Edgbaston
Birmingham
B5 7RN
0845 872 3440
Charity Number 1000598
http://www.samm.org.uk

Missing People UK
Telephone 0500 700 700
http://www.missingpeople.org.uk/